C000173409

STUART MCHARDY is a writer, occasio
been actively involved in many asp
adult life – music, poetry, language,
in Edinburgh for over a quarter of
illustrious positions including Director of the Scots Language Resource
Centre in Perth and President of the Pictish Arts Society, McHardy is
probably proudest of having been a member of the Vigil for a Scottish
Parliament. He is a prolific author and has published books on many
subjects, including *Strange Secrets of Ancient Scotland*, *Tales of Whisky
and Smuggling*, *The Wild Haggis an The Greetin-faced Nyaff*, *Scotland:
Myth, Legend and Folklore* and *Edinburgh and Leith Pub Guide*, the latter
a truly erudite opus. Often to be found in the bookshops, libraries and
tea-rooms of Edinburgh, he lives near the city centre with the lovely (and
ever-tolerant) Sandra and their talented son Roderick.

Tales of Bonnie Prince Charlie and the Jacobites

STUART McHARDY

Luath Press Limited

EDINBURGH

www.luath.co.uk

First published 2012

ISBN: 978-1-908373-23-6

The paper used in this book is recyclable. It is made from
low chlorine pulps produced in a low energy, low emission manner
from renewable forests.

Printed and bound by
Bell & Bain Ltd., Glasgow

Typeset in 10.5 point Sabon
by 3btype.com

Contents

Introduction

ONE OF THE MOST romanticised periods of Scottish history is the Jacobite period, which started with Claverhouse raising a Highland army to fight for the Stewarts in 1689 and ended in the years after the Battle of Quiberon Bay in 1759. That battle saw the last gasp attempt by Prince Charles Edward Stewart to regain the crown of his ancestors for the Stewart dynasty. He was part of a planned French invasion of England which was thwarted by the defeat of the French Navy at Quiberon Bay. Up to that point, the possibility of a Stewart return was still strong, though British history has consistently insisted that the Jacobite cause was finished after the wild slaughter of Culloden on 16 April 1746. In truth, many Scots were sure there would be another rising, and there were many Jacobites who 'stayed out' in the Highlands carrying on a low level guerrilla campaign into the mid 1750s. The tales here of the Seven Stalwart Men and Gypsy Donald reflect that period, which still awaits proper study by historians.

The standard story is that the Rising, or rebellion, of 1745 which, while it saw several victories over the British Army, ended in disaster at Culloden, was a doomed adventure led by the charismatic but fatally flawed Prince Charles Edward Stewart. Bonnie he certainly was, and charismatic and brave, but generations of Scots, disinclined to accept the chocolate box portrayal of the handsome, charming Prince, have been encouraged to think of him as little more than a bumbling fool, who soon turned to drink and debauchery after the loyal sacrifice of his supporters came to nothing at Culloden. I was one of them. However, having spent many years not just searching out stories of the period after the '45, but doing considerable historical research, I have come to change my mind about Bonnie Prince Charlie. Headstrong he certainly was, and in the campaign of the '45, horrendously inexperienced, and capable of both arrogance and duplicity. But we should remember that he was a young man, just 24 years old, who showed great courage, the ability to learn and a great deal of what we might now call stickability. He became an icon of Romanticised Scottish culture even in his own lifetime. The failure of the government's reward of £30,000 to tempt any Scot, no matter their own political or religious leanings, to betray him, speaks volumes about both the Prince and the Scotland of the time.

While it is true that Scotland was, at best, little more to him than a tactical pawn in his struggle to gain the British throne, he did not give up after the horrors of Culloden and his subsequent six months on the run in the Highlands, totally divorced from the life of luxury he had been born into. He returned to the Continent and continued to plan for the eventual overthrow of the Hanoverian dynasty. It was only after the collapse of the final attempt in 1759 that he became embittered and began to turn into the bloated drunk that British propaganda was so happy to publicise. For there is no doubt that from the British perspective, telling us that the Jacobite cause was over by 1746 was handy indeed. But just as the attempt to portray it as a purely Highland rebellion was false – there were more Lowland than Highland troops in the truly Scottish Jacobite army – the reality is that Jacobite plotting continued well into the later years of the 18th century and the hold that Jacobitism had, and still has, on Scottish culture shows that 'official' history does not often touch people's hearts.

This volume contains stories that are based on the historical record and others which have come down through traditional story-telling. And it is the traditional stories that led to me uncovering much of what has been suppressed about the period. For the truth is that the Highlands of Scotland and much of the Lowlands were under British Army occupation until the mid 1750s. This is not what one would expect if the Jacobite threat was truly over after 1746. The records of the British Army garrisons still exist though it may be considered somewhat surprising that some of them have never been published and to date no one has thought to bring all of the diverse material together for scholars to study. History is often said to be written by winners, but that doesn't stop the losers telling stories to one another based on what they knew really happened. And for many Scots in the Jacobite army, the fight for the Stewarts was a fight for Scotland, and though they gave their support to the Prince and his father they cared little for England or Britain.

At a time when we at last have a Scottish Government again, it is refreshing to see their commitment to teaching Scottish history in our schools – something that until 2010 was optional – now we just need to make sure that it is actual Scottish history we teach our children and not the watered down and politically correct versions of it that have been included in so-called British history. In that respect, the stories of our ancestors passed on in Gaelic and Scots may still have a great deal to teach us.

Stuart McHardy
Edinburgh/Dun Edain/Embra
2012

Bonnie Prince Charlie in London

ON 4 DECEMBER 1745 at the head of his Jacobite army, Prince Charles Edward Stewart had reached Derby, 115 miles from London. Intent on getting to London and seizing the throne, he was thwarted by his own Council who had been tricked into believing that there was a British army between the Scottish Jacobites and the capital city. Frustrated by the continuing non-appearance of French troops, whom Charlie had repeatedly said would come, and worried at being so far from their Scottish base, his commanders were in no mood to try and fight their way to London. And so, to Prince Charles' disgust, the Jacobite army turned and headed back to Scotland where, after defeating another British army at Falkirk, they finally blundered into the slaughter of Culloden Moor on 16 April 1746. After that the young prince was on the run in the Scottish Highlands and islands for nearly six months, laying the basis for so many of the stories that have been told ever since. Despite the fact that the British Government put a price of £30,000 on his head, an absolute fortune back then, no one would turn him in, even Scots who weren't Jacobites themselves helped in his eventual escape. But the young man was frustrated by his failure to regain the throne for his father and many in Scotland were ready for his return – it would be different next time they thought.

But Charles never came back to Scotland, for although he had been deeply touched by the loyalty and bravery of the Scots his real interest was in England and, specifically, London. He believed that if he could gain control of London and play his cards right that the people of England would come out in his support. He already had the support of at least half of the Scots and Scotland had only ever been a pawn in a greater game. And we should remember that the Jacobite cause was supported by many of the great powers of Europe.

At one time or another, Charles or his father had been dealing with France, Prussia, Russia, Spain and Sweden, all of whom had an interest in curbing the power of Britain. As far as Charles and his father were concerned, Culloden was only one defeat in a campaign that still had a long way to run, and would end up in victory for the Jacobite cause.

The problem was that Charles and his father James did not see eye to eye. Charlie was a brave and charismatic figure and always saw himself as a man of action. He had a tendency to rashness, while his father, a much colder, even insipid character, moved slowly and always planned for the long term. In the years after Culloden, the young man increasingly went his own way and made his own plans, often not even informing his father of what he was going to do.

Meanwhile, there were still many people in England who supported the Jacobite cause and, as always, there were those who would wait to see which way the wind blew before they showed their hand. Jacobite plotting was rife. Even the common people got into the act – whenever there was a riot in London, a not uncommon experience and often caused by such mundane matters as the price of bread, there would be those who called out for the return of the Stewarts. And at the so-called higher levels of society, there were certainly plenty of people, and not just Catholics, who saw their interests as being better served if they could bring the Stewarts back.

Religion however, was still of primary importance. As long as the Stewarts were Catholic there was little chance of widespread support. England was a defiantly proud Protestant country and the persecution of Catholics was seen as their just desserts for centuries of corruption in their Church and their subservience to a foreign Pope. By 1750, Charles, now approaching his 30th birthday, was no longer the callow young man who had led his Scottish army almost to the gates of London. He had learned a hard lesson and his youthful, even Romantic fervour for his father's, and his own, cause, had been replaced by a more practical approach. No one had ever doubted his courage but in 1750 he set his mind on doing something that was truly breathtaking.

He decided that if he was to gain back the British throne for his father and his family, he had to have as much support from the people of Britain as possible, and so he would have to renounce Catholicism. This was a dangerous course indeed, for the support of France and Spain, such as it had been, and the steady help from the Pope, was always influenced by the wish to see England returned to the fold of the Catholic Church. But Charles, though older and perhaps a bit wiser, was no less headstrong than he had always been, and was dead set on this course of action.

Now ever since he was a young man Charles had been the target of British Intelligence. On several occasions, like his father before him, he had narrowly missed attempted assassination and there was no doubt that the Jacobites were deeply infiltrated with spies. The most famous of these was Alastair Ruadh MacDonnell of Glengarry, a.k.a. Pickle the Spy, who was reporting directly to the British Government from the late 1740s onwards. Never exposed during his lifetime, Glengarry was at the very heart of the Jacobite cause, with easy access to both Charles and his father. However even Pickle did not realise what Charles was up to in 1750. By now Charles was used to travelling incognito, and his time in the Scottish mountains in 1746 had made him quite used to going without the luxuries of life as a Prince. He had no need for great retinues of followers or servants, nor did he have to constantly eat and drink only the most sumptuous fare.

In the summer of 1750, Prince Charles Edward Stewart, sworn enemy of the Hanoverians and the focus of so much government activity, was in London. He had come over from Antwerp with Colonel Brett, a loyal Jacobite, travelling incognito. He had known that there were quite a few of the leading families of English society who were still staunch Jacobites and that he would have no trouble in meeting up with these loyal, if secret supporters. Charles' attempts at secrecy were so effective that his friends did not know he was coming. The evening he arrived he went straight to the London House of Lady Primrose, who he was sure would be delighted to welcome him. Lady Primrose was playing cards with several friends when Charles entered the room unannounced. Looking up from the table one of the ladies said,

'That young fellow there looks a lot like the Prince over the Water.'

Luckily, Lady Primrose had the presence of mind to carry on playing cards and merely smiled. Her heart must have been pounding as she played on and one wonders what she said to the Prince later on. That the lady should notice him was hardly surprising as there were many grand houses in London that had likenesses of the Prince; pictures, silhouettes and even busts.

Simply ignoring the possibility that he might be recognised, Charles went out one day with his companion Colonel Brett, who had come with him from France, to take a look at the Tower of London. This was a recce mission because Charles was thinking of launching a direct attack on the stronghold, at that time the main military post in the city. Once he had command of it he was sure he could rally sufficient support from amongst the population to take over the city, then the whole country.

Brett was an experienced military man and said to the Prince,

'I believe sire, that if we wish to take this place the best plan would be to blow in one of the gates with a petard, then have our men rush in and overpower the garrison. If done with surprise it should be very effective,'

'I think you are right Colonel Brett, and we can have a good start to restoring things to their natural order,' replied the Prince.

The pair of them then casually strolled off. In fact plans were laid to do something along those lines over the next couple of years, though they came to nothing due to MacDonnell of Glengarry informing the government. However, Charles was not just on a recce. While he was in London, staying with Lady Primrose, a 'committed Jacobite', as he later wrote in his memoirs, he did something else of an eminently practical nature. In order to appeal to the majority of the English people, and not just the aristocracy and gentry, who would never under any circumstances accept a Catholic on the throne, he formally renounced his old religion and was admitted to the Anglican

Communion, by the vicar at St Martin in the Fields church. There are those who see this as nothing more than cynical, political posturing but there is no doubt that it was practical. Its timing however was, like so many other Jacobite actions, a bit off. If he had done this before his march into England at the head of a Scottish Army it may well have been effective, but, despite all the ongoing plots, there was little real chance of anything dramatic happening to further his cause at this time.

After a week or so in London, which included a two-day visit to meet with more Jacobite supporters in Oxfordshire, the Prince headed back to the Continent and, to all intents and purposes, disappeared from view for many months. His courage was not in doubt but, as ever, his judgement and timing certainly were. Nearly a decade later he was part of an attempted French invasion, which was defeated at the naval battle of Quiberon Bay in 1759, by which time he had returned to the arms of the Catholic Church, finally seeing off the faint last hope of a Jacobite restitution. However, his courage in visiting London and his attempts at coming to terms with the political realities which faced him make a mockery of the drunken buffoon he was portrayed as. After Quiberon Bay though, he truly was a broken man.

For Love of the Prince

ON HIS WAY SOUTH towards Edinburgh in September 1745, Prince Charlie had stopped with his army in Dunblane. In the town, he stayed in Strathallan's Lodgings in Millrow. One of the servant lasses there, Effie, was given the task of polishing his boots. Late at night after the Prince was asleep she came into his room to get the boots. Looking on the sleeping Prince her heart was filled with emotion and she could not bear to tear herself away. So she sat and polished his boots by the light of a candle. In the morning he awoke to see her still sitting there gazing at him wide-eyed. He reached out his hand towards her but she flushed and fell to her knees, still holding one of his boots.

'Come lass, and take my hand,' he smiled at her.

Effie could not bring herself to speak or even take the offered hand and simply contented her self with kissing his boot her face bright red and her eyes glistening.

'What is wrong lass,' he went on, 'are you scared of me?'

'Och no, my Prince. Och no that's not it at all. I am scared to my heart for you. You are going against the English and there are ten of them for every one of your own men. I fear for you my Prince.' She lowered her head and muffled a sob. 'You need not worry, my dear,' the Prince said, 'once I have gone into England there are many there who will come forward to support my father's cause. Do not worry yourself.'

She got to her feet, put down the boot she had been holding and curtsied to the Prince before scampering from the room. Charles Edward Stewart smiled to himself. This was a good sign, he thought, that even the servants are supporting us. However he had much on his mind and soon forgot all about Effie.

In January of the following year the Jacobite army came to Dunblane again. This time, even though they had just defeated another British Army under General Hawley at Falkirk, they were in retreat. The troops were grim-faced and tired looking. Behind them came the great army of the Duke of Cumberland, set on destroying what he saw as a treasonous rebellion by ingrates and savages. And as they came they looted and pillaged at will. As far as the Duke was concerned, all of these Scots were traitors to his father and deserved whatever they got. He was already, even at the young age of 24, a man of brutal simplicity and utter arrogance. He too came to Dunblane and stayed overnight in the town. In the morning, two men who had been caught stealing from the army baggage train were brought before him in his lodgings. They were a rough-looking pair, both dressed in the simple hodden grey that was almost a uniform for the common people of the time. Both of them were firmly held by a soldier on each side.

'Right' he said, pointing at one of the men, 'What is your name?'

'B-B-B-Brown, Your Highness,' stuttered the man,

'Ah, good. Brown,' said the Duke, 'that is a good English name. We have many Browns in our troops.' He smiled and turned to his aide-de-camp, 'Let this man go free.'

The aide-de-camp nodded to the soldiers holding Brown and he was marched out of the room.

'Now you,' he barked, pointing at the remaining man, 'what is your name?'

'My name is McNiven Sire,' replied the man, bowing his head.

'McNiven, McNiven,' roared the duke, 'That is a filthy thieving Highland name. Take him out and hang him.'

McNiven's head shot up and looked at the Duke who waved his hand and as the man's legs collapsed under him with fear, he was dragged out by the soldiers. They dragged him to a nearby tree and with no further ceremony strung him up as his companion looked on, a free man.

Returning to his breakfast as if nothing had happened Cumberland calmly finished his meal. Then he stepped outside and mounted his magnificent grey charger.

Waving to his officers to follow him he headed off eastwards along Millrow. As he went he passed by Strathallan's Lodging. Just as he got there a figure appeared in a window above him. It was Effie. In her hands she had a pan of boiling oil. Quickly she leaned out of the window and tipped the pan. The searing liquid poured down missing Cumberland by a couple of inches. It didn't miss his horse. The poor creature let out a terrified squeal and reared up, throwing his rider into the dirt. As he sprawled in the street the officers behind him started shouting, 'After her, after her. Surround the building.'

Soldiers battered down the door of the Lodgings as others ran in either direction to get round the back of the house. Boots thundered up the stairs to the room where the potential assassin had stood. There was no-one there. By the time the rest of the soldiers reached the back of the house Effie had made her escape by ducking into the underground culvert through which the Mannie Burn ran to the Allan Water and escaped into open countryside. Behind her, the troops fanned out through the houses in either side of Strathallan's Lodging smashing doors and windows as they went. They found nothing and proceeded to wreck the three houses. Things would have been even worse for Dunblane had not Cumberland himself ordered his men to stop. He had given his word to the local Laird, Drummond, a staunch Hanoverian, that Dunblane would not be torched, and despite the attempted assault, he stuck to his word. As for Effie, she got clean away. Once all the troubles had settled down she married a wealthy local farmer and lived a long and happy life, giving birth to several children, but never forgetting the effect Prince Charlie had on her in her youth.

There has long been a local tradition that Prince Charlie left a special present behind him in Dunblane. A present that nine months later came into the world as a healthy baby boy, who went on to become a minister of religion in Glasgow and who never denied his parentage.

The Ultimate Sacrifice

MAJOR JAMES LOCKHART of Cholmondeley's Regiment was captured by the Jacobites at the Battle of Falkirk. He soon managed
to escape by bribing a guard, and headed back to England. He was
in action at Culloden in April and about a month and a half later
he arrived in Glenmoriston at the south-west shore of Loch Ness,
with a company of Redcoats. As the soldiers came into the glen itself
they passed a field where three men were busy harrowing. They were
John MacDonald and Hugh Fraser, men in their 60s, and Hugh's
son James, who had never set foot more than a mile or two outside the glen. They were simply going about their business and
bothering no one when Lockhart ordered his men to shoot them.
No word of warning, no threatening behaviour towards the
Redcoats, no suggestion that any of them had even been rebels, just
the simple command to kill them. Leaving the bodies lying where
they fell, the government troops headed further into the glen.

The troops then came to the farm of Grant of Dundreggan and
Lockhart had him dragged out of his house before his family.

'Right,' he barked at Grant, 'You will now gather up all the
cattle in this area and bring them here to me.'

Grant was sent off with a group of soldiers accompanying him
while the rest of the troops went on a rampage of looting and
destruction through the glen, burning houses and destroying crops,
all without any suggestion that the people being thus persecuted had
any Jacobite sympathies. Lockhart picked the most comfortable
house in the glen for his own headquarters, simply turning out the
women and children who lived there onto the hillside. His men
similarly took over those houses that took their fancy, throwing
the occupants out to fend as they might. All that night the glen was
filled with the cries of bewildered children, the shrieks of women who
had been assaulted, and worse, the shouts of soldiers moving through
the flickering shadows cast by the burning houses. Many of the sol-

diers were drunk, making free with the whisky and beer they found as they went about their evil work. For many of the Glenmoriston people, it was as if all at once they had been thrust into Hell itself, while still alive.

The following morning Lockhart went back to Dundreggan and hearing that Grant had not managed to gather in all of the glen's cattle, he showed his true character. He had Grant stripped naked, tied hand and foot and then as he lay on the ground near his own front door he had his men bring the bodies of the three men shot the previous day and had them hung by their feet from a nearby tree. It was only the intercession of one Captain Grant of Loudon's Regiment that stopped Lockhart killing Grant there and then and he satisfied himself with burning the house at Dundreggan. He then stripped Grant's wife of her rings and her clothes!

Around the same time one of the Frasers was making his way back from visiting the Presbyterian minister at Kilmorack further up the glen. Seeing the way things had been going he had asked the minister to write him a paper stating that he had not been a rebel, that he was a Presbyterian and that he was loyal to the house of Hanover. He was coming through a stream towards the soldiers waving the paper from the minister when he was shot dead by them.

So they advanced westwards along the glen, burning and pillaging as they went. Women were stripped of their clothing and raped, both young and old, and even a couple who were quite obviously pregnant. Houses were burned indiscriminately and every piece of livestock rounded up and sent to Fort Augustus. Men, women and children fled into the hills and as the destruction went on some of them died from exposure. One detachment of the troops were heading up the glen towards *Ceann-na Croc*, a great rock at the foot of the northern slopes of *Beinn na Eoin* which overlooks the river Moriston when they spotted Roderick MacKenzie. Like many of his kin he had been out in the '45, but he stood apart from all the other Jacobites because of one particular fact. He was the same age, height and build, had the same colouring and the same shape of face as Prince Charles Edward Stewart. It was something that was remarked on constantly through the heady times of 1745 and 1746. After the disbanding of the Jacobite Army at Ruthven Barracks he headed back to his own country around Glenmoriston where, like many others, he was forced to hide out in the hills. Sometimes he would hide in one of the caves in the locality, sometimes creep into barns or outhouses, at others he would build a simple shelter in the woods. Sometimes he had been forced to sleep on the side of a hill in the cold air of the mountain nights. This was not as bad as it sounds for the plaid that most Highlanders wore provided a warm blanket once it was taken off and unfolded. Rebels like Roderick were back in their own clan lands and had relations living in the clachans and small villages that were being methodically searched and pillaged by the Redcoats and they had their own information network.

So it was that Roderick had heard just a day or so earlier that the Prince himself was somewhere around Glenmoriston heading for the west coast where he hoped to get on board a ship that would take him to France.

He was greatly distressed to hear this, as the area was covered with roaming groups of British soldiers and when later that same day he saw some of the Redcoats in the glen below him, he knew what he had to do. He leapt from his hiding place in a small copse of trees and began to head none too quickly on a course parallel to the soldiers. It was only a minute or so before he was seen and when he heard the shout, 'Hold fast, who goes there?'. He began to run off up the glen.

The soldiers immediately gave chase. He ran as far as the great rock of *Ceann-na-Croc* where he turned to face them, sword in hand. He was an able swordsman but, outnumbered as he was – about 12 to one – he could not hope to last long. He had no intention of surrendering. After receiving half a dozen minor blows, but sorely wounding a couple of the Redcoats, he at last took a blow straight through his chest. He knew it was a fatal one and as he slumped to the ground he had just enough breath to gasp, 'Alas, alas you have killed your prince.' He then fell dead at the feet of the soldiers who all stood back at these words.

Some of them were worried that they had committed regicide, for the idea that there was something almost superhuman about royalty still held sway in many minds, but the sergeant in command spoke up.

'Never fear, men,' he said, 'this has been a good days' work. This man was a pretender to the throne and a traitor to the true king. We have faithfully fulfilled the orders of the legal king and I am sure we will be well rewarded.'

He then gave orders for the head of the corpse to be cut off and the body buried close to the great rock of *Ceann-na-Croc*. Now in those days taking heads was a common means of identifying the dead so none of the soldiers thought much about it. Word of the death of the Prince went like wildfire round the government troops in and around Glenmoriston and all search parties were recalled. They had caught their prey and the commanders were sure that this would put a stop to all rebel activity. The stragglers in the hills who didn't surrender once they heard their leader was dead, could be picked off at their leisure. They reckoned that the campaign was effectively over. The local people knew different, for a few of them were allowed to see the head of the supposed Prince to let them understand that any further resistance to the Redcoats was futile. Of course it had the opposite effect. All were proud, but saddened, by the brave death of Roderick Mackenzie but they knew fine well that it gave the fugitive Prince an increased chance of escaping to France and maybe, just maybe, returning at a later date to raise the clans again. The head was taken to the local commander in Fort Augustus and it was shown to MacDonald of Kingsburgh who confirmed that it was the Prince. However, this did not convince the Duke of Cumberland who took the head with him when he went to London.

Richard Morison, valet to the Prince, was in Carlisle prison under sentence of death and Cumberland sent for him to be brought to London. Like many of the Jacobite prisoners he had been badly treated, badly fed and had fallen ill. By the time he could be brought to London the head had rotted beyond recognition and there was little point in even showing it to the poor man. Word had got out however that Prince was still alive and that the head had been that of a loyal follower who had sacrificed himself for Prince Charlie. This combined with the ongoing failure of the £30,000 reward to tempt anyone into betraying the Prince served only to increase the brutality with which the Redcoats treated the Highlanders.

It was quite a few weeks before word came to the troops in Glenmoriston that they had been fooled, but it was too late, the Prince had made the coast and embarked on the *Heureux* for France. Roderick's ultimate sacrifice also saved Richard Morison's life, for after being taken under sentence of death from Carlisle, once he reached London he was given a pardon and allowed to make his way safely to France.

Today, Mackenzie's Cairn marks the scene of Roderick's brave last stand, about half a mile east of the confluence of the Moriston and Doe rivers.

Seven Stalwart Men

WHEN PRINCE CHARLES was on the run with the price of £30,000 on his head he had help from a variety of people. None of them were more important than those who have come down in tradition as the Seven Men of Glenmoriston. Patrick Grant, Hugh, Alexander and Donald Chisholm, Alexander MacDonald, Gregor McGregor and John MacDonald who sometimes passed himself off as a Campbell, had all been in the Jacobite Army. They had returned to their native Glenmoriston after the disbandment at Ruthven and had seen the betrayal and slaughter of friends and relations, the destruction of their homes and the loss of their property at first hand. They made a vow to stand together against the Redcoats till the last drop of their blood. All swore this oath on the blade of their dirks, the most solemn oath a Highlander could make, and began what we nowadays call a guerrilla campaign against the government soldiers. In addition to having been raised in the warrior traditions of the Highland clans they had all served for some time in the Independent Highland Companies that had been raised in the 1730s. When they heard that the prince had raised his standard in Glenfinnan, some of them were still serving, and had immediately deserted and gone to join their kinsmen in the ranks of the Jacobites.

From the point of view of the government they were deserters and there would have been no point in them surrendering to be shot, but what made them become raiders was more to do with the carnage that spread through the Highlands after Culloden than any fear for their own lives. They formed a tight-knit and highly efficient fighting band, for their small numbers were offset by their knowledge of the ground and their extensive knowledge of the enemy's tactics. Like all successful guerrillas, they also had the support of the local population, though due to government raids there was often little they could do to help the Seven Men of Glenmoriston.

However, they could still hunt for deer and they were adept at picking up provisions belonging to the army they had once been part of. Throughout all of this, their greatest hatred was reserved for those of their own kind who acted for the government. The government had great need of Gaelic-speaking natives as there were whole straths and glens where no-one understood a word of English, or even Scots.

They hid out in *Uamh Ruaraidh na Silg* , the cave of Roderick the Hunter in one of the wild corries round the headwaters of the River Doe. This wild country to the north of Glenmoriston was ideal for their purposes. With nothing other than animal tracks through the heather, woods and scrub, it would be folly for anything short of a small army to pursue them, particularly as the red coats of the soldiers would make easy targets for the Seven Men of Glenmoriston.

Now, they might have been living out in a wild part of the country but they all knew how to live off the land and now and again they even had a treat or two. They were watching from the hills overlooking Loch Cluanie when they saw a party of seven Redcoats, led by a man they knew as Alexander MacPherson from Skye, with a pair of heavily laden horses. This small detachment of soldiers were on their way from Glen Elg to Fort Augustus with officers' provisions. They were easy pickings for the Glenmoriston lads. They made their way to a suitable spot and waited behind some boulders, as the column approached. Once they were in range, three of them fired off a volley and two of the Redcoats fell dead. The other four then fired and the surviving soldiers and MacPherson took off at a run towards the east, not even looking back behind them.

They came down the hillside to find what they had acquired. Apart from some fine wheaten bread, canned meats and sweetmeats there were four large leather hampers which were padlocked shut. What could this be but gold?

It was a simple matter to prise the padlocks off with their dirks and they pulled the lids off and looked in. There was no gold. The hampers were instead full of bottles of wine. They buried the dead soldiers, took their weapons and, carrying the food and wine, set off back to their cave slapping the horses to send them off in the same direction as the soldiers had fled. Now they might have been disappointed but as Grant said in later years, 'Well at least we lived like princes for the next few days.'

It was only a couple of weeks after this when they saw a man crossing the area known as *Feith Bob*, Robert's Bog. They all recognised him as Robert Grant, a native of Strathspey who had come into the area working as a translator for the Army. There was no hesitation and the man was shot and killed from a distance. The collaborators were no more than traitors to their own kind as far as the men of the cave were concerned and as a warning to others they beheaded Grant and stuck the head in the cleft of a tree close by the roadside on Loch Cluanie between Innerwick and Duncathick. The people of the area knew fine well what this grisly sight conveyed, and those who did not directly support the Seven Men in their activities would now think more than twice about speaking to the government representatives in the area!

It was only three days after killing Robert Grant that Patrick Grant heard that a detachment of soldiers had taken his uncle Patrick's cattle and were taking them by the recently built Wade Road through Glenmoriston. This was a direct challenge to him and his companions and they decided to take a hand in the matter. The troops, a combined force of regular soldiers and Highlander militia raised from clans loyal to the Hanoverian cause, with three officers and about 60 men accompanying the same number of cattle, were already well on the road and by the time the seven men caught up with them they were approaching the hill of Lundie. The rebels took a position on the side of the hill above the road and called out to the men below,

'Hand over those cattle now or it will be the worse for you.'

Now the soldiers heavily outnumbered the Highlanders but their officer could not be absolutely sure that the small group he could make out on the hill above were all that there were. Perhaps there were others in the heather. So he decided to play things safe. He sent Donald Fraser, a Gaelic-speaking militiaman up the hill to talk to the rebels.

'The Lieutenant has said that if you are prepared to give up your weapons and surrender,' he called out, 'he will make sure that you are shown the utmost mercy and royal clemency.'

This was met with hoots and jeers and Patrick Grant pointed his cocked weapon directly at him. 'We'll just see who needs mercy when the rest of the lads catch up. They are not far behind us. Now tell that southron fool to leave the cattle and get off to wherever you are going. It will be the worse for many of you if you do not.'

As Fraser turned to go back down the hill to report to his lieutenant, Patrick spoke again. 'Wait. Just stand there and don't move.'

Keeping his gun levelled he came up to Fraser and stuck his free hand in the militiaman's knapsack, pulling out a half-pound of tobacco.

'Very nice,' he said sniffing the plug, 'You can go now' he went on, stuffing the tobacco into his sporran.

The troops headed on their way up the hill, their officers had no intention of giving in to such a puny force. So the seven carried on a flanking movement above them firing in sequence so there was a continuous series of musket balls flying over their heads. Still they pressed on, even after a few of their number been wounded and they began to return fire. The advantage of tartan against heather and scrub had always been that it served as a form of camouflage and as the Highlanders were also sure-footed and fast, none of them were injured. Things carried on like this for a short while, until suddenly the firing from above stopped, and as the officers watched the seven indistinct figures up on the hill ran forwards and over a rise in the hill. Soon they were out of sight. Not for long.

As the soldiers and the cattle came up the track, they saw that the road went through a narrow pass. And from the rocks on either side of the pass muskets began to flash. The soldiers were not used to this kind of warfare and despite their officers' best efforts, some of them turned and ran. The cattle were spooked and broke out in all directions.

The officers regrouped their men back down the road as the

cattle scattered through the heather making a great noise. Another of the militiamen was sent forward to parley with the rebels. This time it was an officer, a MacDonald, who approached.

'What is it you are wanting?' shouted Hugh Chisholm, 'We have said all that we are wanting to say.'

'I have been sent by the Commanding Officer to ask if you are mad taking on this many of the king's troops?' came the reply.

'Well and if your king came here now he would get just the same,' Gregor MacGregor spoke.

'Well then,' MacDonald replied, 'I have been told to offer you clemency again, but don't believe it for a minute. If you surrender you will be bound and gagged and carried off for trial.' MacDonald had been sickened by the behaviour he had witnessed over the previous months and had a growing sympathy for the rebels.

'If the firing starts again, aim for the taller of the two officers. Kill him and the others will run. I will try and keep my men away from the Redcoats and we will fire in the air. I will go back now and tell them you intend to fight for the cattle. Good luck.'

The Glenmoriston men looked at each other as he went back to the main force. This was a turn up. So they decided to wait and see what would happen.

MacDonald returned to the other soldiers and there made it very clear that the rebels had no intention of either letting the detachment pass or leaving themselves, and were prepared to die to try and get the cattle. Having seen some of his men run off and not being too sure of the loyalty of the militia men, the commanding officer decided that there would be no point in attacking the men in the pass. He might succeed in killing them but given their position and clear intention it would be a costly victory. If they tried to drive the cattle back they would be presenting clear targets to the well-hidden marksmen behind them. The upshot was that the officer made the best of a bad job and decided to hand the cattle over.

He ordered MacDonald to get his militiamen to gather up the cattle to hand over to the their adversaries. In the course of this being done two of the Glenmoriston nipped out from their positions and captured two of the militiamen – and it might not be pushing things to think that the militiamen put up no great struggle.

The Glenmoriston lads then called for another parley and demanded that they be given some of the detachment's provisions in exchange for their hostages. This further enraged the already furious commanding officer but he was forced to agree and a short while later the entire detachment of troops headed back the way they had come, leaving the Seven Men of Glenmoriston with the entire herd of cattle, as well as a bonus horse laden with provisions! Through their knowledge and experience of the lay of the land, and sheer bloody-mindedness, the seven of them had got the better of 60 of their enemy.

Not long after this on 28 July, the weather had turned bad and Alexander Chisholm and the two MacDonalds were sitting by the fire in their cave with the rain pouring down, their companions having gone off foraging, when they heard a shout. Grabbing their weapons they peered out into the rain to see a distant cousin of John MacDonald's from Glengarry. He was welcomed in out of the rain and offered some mutton and whisky.

'Thanks lads,' he said, 'but not at this moment. I have been out on the hill with Glenaladale and his brother John MacDonald of Borrodale and another young gentleman for the past three days. We are all sore in need of food and shelter, particularly the young gentleman. Can I bring them in?'

'Of course you can,' said Chisholm, 'we have plenty of food, though I am sorry to say we don't have any spare clothes. The fire is good and warm though and we are safe here.'

So the man from Glengarry went back up onto the hilltops above Glen Dho where his party had spent a miserable night in a damp cave that was little more than an overhanging cliff, and a short while later returned with his companions.

As they came into the cave, John MacDonald leapt to his feet, his face turning bright red. His companions reached for their arms and then looked at who had come into their cave. They too had thought the unnamed visitor might have been young Clanranald, they had not expected it to be Charles Edward Stewart.

'Your Highness,' stuttered John, 'it is sorry I am to see you in this state and I hope to see you in better soon. I last saw you at the head of the troops on Glasgow Green, and, and,' his voice caught with emotion for a second, then he went on, 'and I thought then I would follow you wherever you might lead, but I never thought to see you here. Come in my Prince, come sit by the fire and eat, we have plenty food.'

All three were on their feet as the Prince nodded and smiled, as Glenaladale translated John's words. Nodding again he sat down, clearly exhausted, and the three Glenmoriston men set about giving their guests food and drink. Once they had eaten and had a drink of whisky, it was explained that the party were heading to the west where they had hopes that a French ship was waiting for them off Poolewe. As they hadn't eaten for 48 hours and had had little sleep they were all exhausted, particularly the Prince who, though he could keep up a good pace in the daylight hours, had struggled over the rough ground after dark when they had been forced to do much of their travelling over the previous weeks. So they all lay down on the simple beds of heather and slept peacefully for the first time in quite a while.

In the morning, Glenaladale asked if it would be possible for three of the Glenmoriston lads to take the party on, as their guide was not sure of the country to the west. John MacDonald replied, 'We hear what you are saying but we can do nothing till we have consulted with our companions. We have sworn an oath to stick together till death and we cannot desert them, not even for the Prince himself. You understand?' This last was said with a hard look, and Glenaladale realised that they had sworn the oath on their dirks. Once Charles had been informed of the situation he realised he had to accept it and he asked if they would swear loyalty to him. This, the three of them were happy to do, and though to today's ears the words are somewhat clumsy and archaic there can be no doubt of the sincerity with which this oath was taken. They swore 'That their backs should be to God and their faces to the Devil, and that all the curses the Scriptures did pronounce might come upon them and all their posterity if they did not stand firm with the Prince in the greatest dangers, and if they did discover to any person, man, woman or child – that the Prince was in their keeping, till once his person should be out of danger.' In fact nothing was said about the Prince's sojourn in the hills above Glenmoriston for over a year after he had successfully left the country.

Impressed by these brave and loyal supporters, Prince Charlie proposed that he and Glenaladale should themselves swear, 'that if danger should come upon them they should stand by one another till the last drop of blood.'

The Prince was told with a smile that there was no need for any reciprocal oaths. The Prince then told Glenaladale to tell them that if he was successful in coming into his own inheritance, he would never forget their service. At that, Chisholm said, in Gaelic, that he had heard that Charles II had said something of the sort before he regained his throne and that those he had promised were still waiting. Glenaladale and his brother were a bit put out at this statement and when the Prince insisted they tell him what had been said he replied, nodding, 'I am heartily sorry for that, and I hope I myself will not follow the same measures and you can depend on my word as a Prince.'

A day passed while they waited for the others to return. When at last they came they were leading an ox through the heather and carrying most of a fine stag on their shoulders. It didn't take long for them to be put in the picture. They were all happy to take the same oath as their companions and the ox was slaughtered. Apologies for the lack of salt and bread were made but the Prince said he was more than happy to share whatever was available. Then, however, the discussion turned to what was to be done next. The Prince was most insistent that there was no time to be wasted – he wanted to head west as soon as possible. However, the four who had been out foraging had seen several patrols, and were equally insistent that there was no way anyone could leave the safety of the cave high in the hills for a few days at least. When the Prince tried to command them to his will he was told in no uncertain fashion that he would be tied up to prevent him going for there was no doubt that he would come to harm and they would not, could not, allow that. There was a great deal of tension in the air when Charles Edward Stewart, always known as a man of considerable charm calmed everyone down by saying these words, 'I find Kings and Princes must be ruled by their Privy Council but I believe there is not in the world a more absolute Privy Council than what I have at present, I accept your advice gentlemen.'

So this stay in the hills continued for a few more days, some of them spent in another cave in a nearby corrie – there was no point in not being as careful as possible in the circumstances, the Glenmoriston men told their Prince. While they were still at the head of Corrie Dho, Hugh Chisholm's men went down to get some bread, salt and other food for their guests from John Chisholm whose farm at Fassanacoil had escaped the destruction that had been carried out in so much of the area. Here they were told that one Lieutenant Campbell was in the area. He was only a few miles away with a large herd of cattle that was being driven south. This of course had neither been lifted, nor stolen but appropriated in a totally legal fashion by men in red coats. After returning with this news, he and John MacDonald went off to take a look. They returned a few hours later saying that there was no danger there and the countryside looked clear of troops.

It was now safe to move on. They headed off over the hills to Strathglass and a couple of days later, Glenaladale and MacDonald of Borrodale went on ahead to find out if there was any news of the ship. They returned to where the rest of the company were resting in some shieling huts with the news that two gentlemen had landed from a French ship and headed towards Cameron country round Loch Eil looking for the Prince. So now they had to retrace their steps, with the Seven Men of Glenmoriston spread out around the others as scouts. Messages were sent to Cameron of Clunes to see if a meeting could be arranged. By now they were all sleeping rough and their food was low. Once again though, the Glenmoriston men came through when Patrick Grant brought down a deer at a distance of nearly half a mile.

On 20 August Prince Charles at last met with the men who had come to take him to the waiting ship. Dugald MacCullonoy, as he had insisted on being called while with the Glenmoriston men, was effusive in his thanks and insisted that Patrick Grant come with him till he could find some funds to recompense these loyal men for their troubles. He then took a solemn farewell of them and they headed back to their cave. It was still a while till the Prince managed to get away and a few days later Patrick Grant returned to the Cave of Roderick the Hunter with the truly princely sum of three guineas a man! This was all the money that the Prince could find spare and it was a fair way short of the £30,000 that the government had put on the head of Prince Charles Edward Stewart! The Seven Men of Glenmoriston however, thought that they had the best of the bargain.

They returned to their guerrilla ways and though both Alexander MacDonald and Alexander Chisholm were dead within five years, the others lived on. Most of them though had to leave the area, as the destruction of houses and crops and the removal of cattle had destroyed the simple self-sufficient life style that had sustained the local population for centuries. Many years later, Hugh Chisholm found himself living in Edinburgh where he could always guarantee a meal and a drink by telling of the time he was on the run with Bonnie Prince Charlie. No matter who was in his company, carpenter or lawyer, minister or cobbler, he would only shake hands with his left hand. He was proud to tell all who would listen, 'No man has shaken my right hand since it was shaken by Prince Charles Edward Stewart when he bade me farewell at Achnasoul.'

Defeat in Victory

I fought on land, I fought on sea
At hame I fought ma auntie-o
But I met the Devil an Dundee
On the Braes o Killiecrankie-o.

THIS VERSE FROM the famous Scots song, Killiecrankie, sums up the feelings of a soldier on the government side at the fateful battle of 27 June 1689. The outcome of this battle, if it had been but slightly different, might well have altered the subsequent history not just of Scotland, but the whole British Isles, and perhaps the world. When the English parliament deposed King James VII in 1688 and replaced him with William of Orange the Jacobite cause came into being, dedicated to restoring the House of Stewart to the throne of Britain. One of the most prominent of the early Jacobites was John Graham of Claverhouse, Viscount Dundee. An experienced and able soldier, Claverhouse reminded many of an earlier protagonist of the Stewarts, the Marquis of Montrose, also a Graham and a kinsman of Claverhouse, who had fought for King Charles II in the 1640s and 50s. John Graham was a bit of a romantic and modelled himself on Montrose, though he hoped to escape the fate of his kinsman. He had been executed and, in time-honoured fashion, parts of his body had been sent around the country to be displayed on spikes at the gates into major towns. In his youth, Claverhouse saw the dessicated leg of Montrose displayed at Perth and it seems likely that this grisly sight angered him and thus strengthened his loyalty to the Stewarts. He has gone down in history as one of the great Scottish heroes because of one particular reason, the Battle of Killiecrankie.

By the time of the installation of William of Orange as King in 1689, Claverhouse was already an experienced soldier, having served in the French army in the 1760s. Ironically one of his companions at that time was Hugh Mackay, who ended up commanding the government forces at Kiliecrankie! In 1689 there was a Convention held in Edinburgh to decide which way Scotland was to go. At this point the Treaty of Union had not yet been foisted on the Scottish people, and though the crowns of Scotland and England were conjoined, the two countries were still separate entities. Claverhouse was of course loyal to King James VII, who had been deposed in England, and when the Convention voted to accept William of Orange as their new king he knew what he had to do. As the song Bonnie Dundee puts it,

'To the Lords of Convention
'twas Claverhouse spoke.
Ere the king's crown go down
There are crowns to be broke.'

He left Edinburgh and headed north to raise an army composed almost exclusively of warriors from the Highland clans. On 26 July this Highland force met a British government force under General Mackay at Killiecrankie, a narrow pass through the mountains north of Pitlochry. The two armies appeared to be mismatched – Mackay had four thousand trained soldiers while Claverhouse had half that number of Highlanders who were in no way similar to the disciplined troops of the government. They were however, on home ground and the outcome of the battle between a force of armed clansmen led by a charismatic figure and the disciplined and regimented army troops provided a romantic template for Jacobite song and story for the next century.

Claverhouse's immediate aim as he approached the Pass of Killiecrankie was to get through the pass and head on to Perth. This would allow him to consolidate his hold on Scotland north of the Tay and build up his power base from there. Mackay of course had the explicit task of stopping this from happening.

On the day of the battle itself Mackay had managed to get through the Pass of Killiecrankie itself but found that Graham had taken command of much of the high ground just north of the pass. Throughout the day there were gunshots exchanged between the two forces but Dundee had no intention of letting his Highland troops charge on the enemy while the sun shone in their faces. So it was late in the day before he used the most formidable weapon he had – the Highland charge. This was a well-tested tactic in which the Highlanders would divest themselves of everything but their shirts and weapons and charge down a slope against their enemies. Those who had guns would fire them, drop them and then resort to a tactic that had been honed over centuries of use. In their right hand they carried a broad bladed, double-edged sword, usually with a basket hilt. The left forearm was held through two leather loops on the back of the targe, the Highland leather and wooden shield which had an iron or steel spike, up to a foot long, in its centre, whilst the left hand held that ubiquitous weapon of the Highlander, the dirk, triangular bladed, razor sharp and also up to a foot in length. With the momentum of the charge, the targe would be used to deflect swords, muskets with bayonets, pikes or any other weapon of the man directly in front, while the right hand swept the sword at the man to the right. Once the man in front's weapon was deflected, if he had not been injured by the spike of the targe, the dirk would be used to stab him. It was a brutal and effective form of hand-to-hand combat and for centuries the Highland charge carried all before it. It was a tactic that relied on several factors; the skill of the men with their weapons, their ability to run downhill over rough ground at full speed and, most importantly, the slope to run down. It was a tactic designed for, and perfected in, the glens of the Scottish mountains. It also had the further advantage of being terrifying, a psychological effect that played havoc with enemy resolve, even on the battle hardened Lowland troops of General Mackay at Killiecrankie.

The traditional behaviour of the Highland warrior showed up in other ways that day. Ewen Cameron of Lochiel was leading his own clansmen and was shadowed by the son of his foster-brother. Fostering was the system by which sons of leading families were brought up in the households of other kinsmen. This meant that on top of any brothers of their own, they had the added bonus of foster-brothers, a considerable advantage for those who were destined to become chiefs. It was said that the loyalty of foster-brothers was unsurpassable. Lochiel was in the thick of the battle and realised that his faithful companion was no longer by his side. In a brief break in the hand-to-hand fighting he turned to look around. There a few yards behind him lay his loyal kinsman lying on his back, with an arrow sticking out of his chest. Lochiel ran back to where he lay, knelt down and lifted his head gently.

'Ochone, ochone,' he said, 'they have shot you my good friend.'

'Ach, well,' gasped the dying man, 'I saw that one of those damned government men, a Highlander like ourselves, had nocked his arrow and had you in his sights, I could not let him shoot you Locheil, now could I?' And saying that, he gave a last gasp and died in the arms of his chief. If he had been furious in battle till then, Locheil was now like a berserker of old, and he and his Cameron kin swept through the government forces like a wind of death. It was a costly attack though, for they lost over a hundred men in that fierce battle.

Before the battle itself started Claverhouse had asked Lochiel who should have the victory. Like many Highlanders Lochiel had the gift, or more truly, the curse, of the second sight, the ability to discern the future. His reply was simple, 'He who draws the first blood, shall win the day.'

The Jacobite Army was almost completely made up of Highlanders who had a great respect for the second sight, and those who had the gift of it. Lochiel's words spread through the ranks like wildfire. When his words reached to the contingent from the Grant clan, Grant of Glenmoriston knew what to do.

'Where's Iain Beg?' he cried to his men.

Iain Beg MacRae, famed among his kin for his skill with the gun, was called for and came running to where Glenmoriston stood.

'Here I am,' he said, 'what would you have me do?'

Glenmoriston pointed towards the enemy rank. There riding along the enemy lines was an officer on a white horse.

'Well Iain, does that white horse not make its rider a good target?' he asked with a grim smile.

'Aye so it does,' replied the other. And, lifting his gun to his shoulder he sighted along the barrel. He fired. His aim was good and all the Grants held their breath. Then the rider in the distance threw up his arms, his horse reared and he fell to the earth, dead. All along the Highland line the cheers rang out. The first blood was theirs and they now had no doubt that victory would follow. Who could argue with fate? A nearby well *Fuaran a trupar*, the 'Trooper's Well', was later re-named as such to show where the horseman fell.

Soon the battle was being fiercely fought hand-to-hand over a considerable area. In the pass itself one of Mackay's officers, Brigadier-General Balfour, a Lowland Scot, had seen his men fall around him under the onslaught of the Highland troops. One by one, the men with him fell till at last he was on his own and was forced back against a tree fending off two assailants with his sword. One of these was Alastair Ban Stewart. As the General bravely defended himself against his attackers Alistair Ban's son came up. Seeing the soldier putting up such a good fight against two enemies, he called out in Gaelic. 'Shame, shame on you father, give the brave man his life.'

Alastair Ban and his companion both stepped back, turned and looked at the young man, as Balfour took the opportunity to suck in great breaths of air.

Coming closer the younger Stewart complimented the officer on his skill as a swordsman, in English. Like all Highland lads he had been brought up with the notion of *cothrom na Feinne*, the fair play of Finn McCoul, and Highland tradition had long focused on fighting one on one. In the heat of battle however such niceties were easily forgotten. He had merely been trying to remind his father of the right way of doing things when he called out. The reaction of the Lowlander to this intrusion was not at all what he had expected.

'To hell with you, you Highland dog,' cried Balfour, fired up by the battle conditions as much as his opponents, and he lunged at the young Highlander.

At this, young Stewart moved nimbly to one side and swung his great claymore down on Balfour's collarbone, slicing through his body as far as his waist.

'Now there was a man who did not know when he was well off,' his father said to him before they headed off back to the battle. Not far from the scene of the battle is a large flat stone known as the Balfour Stone where it has been said the unfortunate Brigadier-General was buried afterwards.

A sentry in the government troops had been stationed near the south end of the pass and the first he knew of the outcome of the battle was when he saw a group of Highlanders rushing towards him. He immediately took to his heels and ran for the river Garry. His pursuers were catching up and he was sure that they had him as he was running towards a rock jutting out over the river below in fact one of them had scratched his shoulder with his sword and in his desperation to escape the trooper leapt out from the rock over the river. As he fell on the other side he reached out and grabbed a bush to stop himself falling back. Behind him the Highlanders had stopped and there are those who say that when one of them tried to shoot the fleeing soldier, his companions stopped him, reckoning that his bravery in leaping over the river entitled the soldier to escape, *cothrom na Feinne* still mattered. From then on the local people referred to this spot as the Soldier's Leap.

The government troops were routed, many of them being killed on the battlefield or in the following pursuit, though about 500 of them were taken prisoner. The battle was going well for the Jacobites when Claverhouse stood up in his stirrups to signal his horsemen to charge the government troops of Leven's regiment, who were still standing firm. As he lifted himself up a bullet entered under his raised arm and he was thrown from his horse. He fell to the ground mortally wounded, and even as his men triumphed over their enemies he breathed his last on the heather. With the loss of such a talented and charismatic leader the Jacobite cause itself suffered a terrible blow. A few days later the Highland army were driven back after a fire fight at the town of Dunkeld, about 15 miles south of Killiecrankie, and the rebellion was effectively over. Yet again a Highland army drifted away like smoke into the hills and glens. However, even his death was not enough for some of Claverhouse's enemies and the story was soon doing the rounds that he had in fact been killed by one of his own men, keen to rid the country of Popery and the Stewarts who supported it! Some incurable Romantics also like to believe that beneath his iron breastplate Graham was wearing a Knight Templar's uniform! Stories gather round heroes and in defeating a larger government force only to die in the heather, Claverhouse left a legend that has inspired many a story and song since.

Brass Neck on the Bass Rock

STANDING OFF THE LOTHIAN coast in the Firth of Forth, just opposite North Berwick, is the magnificent Bass Rock. Though nowadays a bird sanctuary, the Bass has had a turbulent history, and no more so than in the late years of the 17th century. When King James was driven from the throne by the English Parliament in 1688 to be replaced by William of Orange the rump of the Scottish Parliament was quick to agree to the change of monarch. Not all Scots, or Englishmen, were happy with the new state of affairs though and while Graham of Claverhouse headed north to raise a Highland army to fight for his king, and close friend, James VII, Charles Maitland, the commandant of the castle on the Bass Rock, held out for the deposed king. It wasn't until 1690 that he was forced to surrender. The castle was then used as a prison, as it had been so often in the past, and four young Jacobites Lieutenant Middleton and ensigns Halyburton, Roy and Dunbar were shut up on the isolated island.

Now many prisoners down the centuries have used the time that lay heavy on their hands to study, to write or to work on physical fitness and there have been those who became talented naturalists during their incarceration, but these lads were made of sterner stuff. Although there were only four of them they resolved to strike a blow for the Stewart cause!

The old, cold building of Bass Rock castle was kept warm by coal fires and when a delivery of coal was brought from the shore they had noticed that all but three or four of the troop garrisoning the castle went down to the jetty to unload the delivery. On 15 June 1691 one such delivery arrived and the majority of the garrison headed down to the jetty, locking three of the four gates on the stairs behind them. Now the castle contained only a sergeant, a gunner and one soldier. They were immediately overpowered by the four Jacobites who then trained one of the castle guns on the working party operating the crane down on the jetty. On shouting down that they had the option to go ashore with the boat or to fight, the officers and men of the working party chose the safer option, and went ashore on the coal boat. The Jacobites now had control of the Bass Rock and raised the flag of King James for all to see.

The next night they were joined by a further four men, Crawford of Ardmillan and his servant and two Irish sailors, Jacobites who had recently made their escape from Edinburgh jail. They had commandeered, or stolen, a small boat further up the Firth of Forth and rowed out under cover of darkness.

News of the taking of the Bass was soon widespread and it was only a matter of time before word got to King James himself, in exile in France. At once he sent a ship with provisions for the now Jacobite garrison. Despite the efforts of the government troops watching from the Lothian shore, the French ship managed to ferry the provisions to the rock, leaving behind a sturdy longboat and the eight men settled into their isolated life. From time to time the old fort on the rock would be bombarded by navy ships but this had little effect – other than giving Middleton and his men the chance to gather the cannonballs to be used in their own guns! Every so often they would go ashore in the longboat during the night to pick up fresh supplies. One night in August, when Middleton and Ardmillan had gone ashore on just such a mission, the longboat was discovered by soldiers and they were stranded.

Back on the Rock, Roy and Dunbar discussed matters with the others and without their leader they thought it might be best to surrender. So Dunbar went ashore in a smaller boat they still had, to see what terms he could negotiate from their enemies. He hadn't long landed at North Berwick when a boat appeared in the river, heading for the Bass. It was Middleton, who was bringing further supplies! Dunbar was imprisoned on shore. Not long before this the Jacobites had sent their own prisoners ashore, leaving less mouths to feed on the rock.

All this time the occupation of the Bass was a daily insult to the new King and his government. All foreign ships coming in to the Forth could see the flag of King James still flying and this was an intolerable situation. Something had to be done. Things got even worse when Middleton fired on a passing Danish ship, forcing it to drop anchor, then going aboard to gather further supplies for his men.

This sheer effrontery caused an immediate reaction. Two ships, the *Sheerness* under Captain Koope, and the *London Merchant* under Captain Orton, were dispatched with orders to bombard the Bass and destroy the fort. For two days the ships and the men in the fort exchanged cannon fire. The result was that the *Sheerness* and the *London Merchant* lost some of their crew and sustained considerable damage to their rigging while their cannonballs caused the Bass garrison no harm at all. Then the two ships limped back to Leith to be repaired.

However, things were becoming more serious for the young Jacobites. A permanent naval presence was set up with the small six-gun *Lion* and a long-boat constantly cruising the waters around the Bass. It seemed only a matter of time now before the men on the Bass would be forced to surrender when their supplies ran out. They had long ago eaten the sheep that used to graze on the rock and were now on heavily reduced rations. Then in August another French ship arrived in the Forth. She was a twelve gun ship and at first the *Lion* stood off as she approached the Bass. Once the supplies were being unloaded, with the help of ten French sailors, the *Lion* made an appearance and attacked the moored French vessel, forcing her to cut her cables and sail off out into the Firth.

The upshot of this was that the ten French sailors were stranded on the bass and with more than double the number of men to feed, supplies soon began to run out. One night soon after, Halyburton rowed ashore in their remaining boat but such was the watch now being kept that he was followed on shore, captured with a local supporter and thrown in prison. The following day the naval long-boat rowed out to the Bass under a white flag to inform the garrison that Halyburton was to be hanged as a traitor.

The same fate awaited the Jacobite he had met on shore, a local man called Trotter. A few days later the sentence was carried out on Trotter, on the beach opposite the rock. A great crowd had gathered and Middleton fired a few cannonballs at them. Though the crowd scattered it did nothing to help poor Trotter whose lifeless corpse was soon swinging in the breeze, clearly visible to the men on the Bass Rock. It now seemed that the game was up. However Middleton was no fool. He had long realised that surrender was inevitable and had put aside a special cache of delicacies and wines that had been landed from the first French ship, all those months before.

He then raised a flag of truce and when the *Lion* approached said he wanted to sue for peace. Before the envoys of the government arrived he carefully deployed hats, coats and muskets to make it appear that he had considerably more men than were in fact on the rock – their numbers never having been accurately ascertained by the watching naval forces.

The envoys were astonished to be fed a sumptuous meal accompanied by the best of French wine, and were totally taken in. Once they had a few glasses of the excellent claret, Middleton put forward his terms. Believing that the castle was still well-stocked, and well-manned, the envoys returned to shore to tell the members of the King's Privy Council in Edinburgh what had been said.

'I want a complete pardon for all of my men, including Halyburton. We are to be given passage to France, and all the monies due to us as soldiers of the true king when we were arrested, are to be paid in full, as are all the expenses we have incurred since taking over the castle. We are to be allowed to go ashore in our own boat with our arms and be granted all the honours of war.'

This was a stupendous piece of bluff, for all that remained in the store room of the Bass was a few pounds of flour. But the bluff worked, and rather than have the constant running sore of a Jacobite presence for all the world to see in the Firth of Forth, the government capitulated.

For sheer brass-neck Lieutenant Middleton has to rank as one of the most remarkable Jacobites ever to fight for the cause.

Duncan the Seeker

IN THE YEARS at the beginning of the 18th century there was a great deal of contact between Jacobites in both Scotland and England and those on the Continent, particularly in the period immediately before 1715. Ships carrying claret from Bordeaux to the ever-thirsty market in Scotland were often used to transport both arms and money. The British Navy did not have enough ships to monitor every vessel that made its way from France to Britain and many got through. Sometimes there were considerable amounts of both gold and weapons but at other times the supplies came in small amounts. Duncan Graham, a Perthshire man, had gone off in the early years of the century to join the Jacobite court in France. Both his parents were dead, he had no brothers or sisters and he was a strong supporter of the cause. He went on to serve in one of the Scottish regiments in the French Army, till in November 1715 he was put in charge of a consignment heading to Britain in a small ship with five fellow Scots. The consignment consisted of a fair amount of gold, swords, muskets and gunpowder, all of which was intended to be distributed amongst Jacobite sympathisers in north-west England. Duncan's intention was to land on the southern shore of the Solway Firth and hide the supplies while he made contact with the men whose names he had been given. He would then help them distribute the money and arms before heading north to join up with the rebellion in Scotland.

As he sailed up through the Irish Sea his ship was spotted by an English cruiser, which immediately gave chase. Luckily Duncan's ship was considerably faster than the Navy one but the chase drove him north of his intended landing place, and by the time they had given the cruiser the slip the ship was sailing up the Firth of Clyde. Now, in those far off times news took time to travel and he was unaware of the current situation of the Jacobite Army. He made landfall by night between Helensburgh and Dumbarton and went ashore to find out how things stood, hoping to hear news of a great Jacobite victory.

He made his way to a local tavern and went in to have a drink.

Before leaving France, he had made sure that he was dressed as plainly as possible and no one paid much attention to him in the tavern. As he sat at a table drinking he heard the story of Mar's debacle at Sheriffmuir and the pathetic surrender at Preston. Clearly there would be little point in looking to find his contacts in the north-west of England. They were likely to be dead or in prison. From what he had heard it was clear that Bobbing John, as the locals scathingly referred to the Earl of Mar, was still at Perth. So, downing his drink, he headed back to the ship. He was in a quandary, from the way the locals had been speaking, some bitterly and others disparagingly, it seemed as if the rising was effectively over. He also realised that the country between him and Perth was liable to be over-run with the red-coated soldiers and Campbell clansmen of the Duke of Argyll's army. Transporting weapons through the countryside would be foolish but maybe he could get the money to Mar. It would be useful for another attempt later. At the very least he would have done something positive for the cause, if he got the money through.

So he and his five companions unloaded the arms and the money before telling the ship's captain to return to France as best he could. They buried the arms and the barrel full of gold not far from the shore and lay down to sleep, wrapped in the blankets they had brought from the ship. The following day Duncan made his way to Dumbarton where he bought a dozen strong leather satchels and headed back to where his friends were. They then distributed the gold between the satchels, and carrying two of them apiece they headed off through the Lennox. They were armed with pistols and swords but they made slow progress as they were desperate not to run into any army patrols. This meant regularly stopping and sending a couple of their number ahead to scout out the land. Progress was slow and there were so many troops about that they were forced to head north towards the Trossachs, hoping to make their way to Perth along the southern edge of the mountains.

They were managing to buy enough food to keep going as they

went but there seemed to be government troops everywhere. However, Duncan was not a man to be put off once he had his mind set, so they soldiered on. Three days later, they had only got as far as the slopes of Ben Ledi overlooking Loch Venachar and it was obvious they cold not carry on as they were. They had seen numerous army patrols over the previous 24 hours and Duncan reluctantly decided they would have to bury the gold, split up and try to get through to Perth one by one. Even if only one of them got through, he might be able to return later with enough of a force to reclaim the gold. So they buried the gold in the shade of a large boulder, ate some of the bread and cheese they had managed to buy that morning, and washed it down with water from the nearby burn. They then set off east, intending to split up within the hour. What they didn't know was that the man who had sold them the bread and cheese that morning had sent word to the local garrison that there was a group of suspicious strangers heading east. They had only gone half an hour from where the gold was buried when they heard a cry from behind them

'Stand in the king's name!'

They turned to see 20 soldiers coming down the shoulder of the hill they had just crossed. They were severely outnumbered but Duncan hardly noticed. All of his disappointment and tiredness disappeared as a wave of rage and hatred against the soldiers swept over him. He turned, whipped out his pistols and fired at the oncoming soldiers. One of them fell and as his companions to began to fire, the soldiers fired a volley at them. Then before he could think, Duncan, sword in hand, was lunging at a large red-faced soldier whose face was as set in hatred as his own. He tried to parry Duncan's lunge but the sword pierced his side just as one of his fellows caught Duncan's shoulder with his bayonet. Duncan hardly noticed as he swung at two more Redcoats who came at him. The skirmish though was short. Outnumbered as they were, there was little hope for Duncan's party, he himself being finally hacked down from behind by the officer in charge, having already sustained a number of serious wounds. As he crashed to the heather, covered in blood his companions threw down their weapons. They were outmatched and to fight on would be to die, and for what? The soldiers tied their arms behind their backs and marched them off, leaving the body of Duncan Graham lying in the heather.

It was late that day when a band of Highlanders, MacIntyres, who had been off taking cattle to market and were heading home towards Strathyre, came upon the body lying in the heather. They had not been in Mar's army but their sympathy was with the Stewarts rather than the Hanoverians, and they realised that this man had been fighting with the soldiers they had seen at a distance, earlier that day. They had been escorting some prisoners and it seemed likely that this man had been one of their party. The man in the front of the group, a stocky dark-haired and bearded man, dressed like his companions in the Highland plaid, knelt down and felt at Duncan's neck for a pulse. It was faint but the man was still alive, if only just. 'Right lads, lets see to his wounds and we'll carry him with us,' he said, adding, 'those German-loving swine didn't even check to see if he was dead.'

They carried him to a cottage, not far off, where one of their kinswomen lived, and left him there to recover. Nursed by the lady of the house for days it seemed as if he would not recover, thrashing about in a fever and his wounds bursting open anew.

It was fully a week before he opened his eyes to find himself inside a black house with a fair-haired woman standing over him with a bowl in her hands. 'Here,' she said, 'I will help you take some of this broth.'

She put the bowl on the edge of the bed and gently lifting his head, gave him small sips of the liquid in a horn spoon. After only a few sips of the venison broth Duncan fell back and once more drifted into sleep, but this time he was more peaceful.

Over the next few months he gradually regained his strength, but he seemed confused. He told his hosts his name but little else, every question meeting with the reply that he was in charge of the King's gold. His mind had clearly been affected by what had happened and even as he grew stronger it became clear that he was brain-damaged.

By the time he was able to walk again many months had passed and the MacIntyres and their neighbours all knew well that he was obsessed with one idea and one idea alone. He said he had to go and get the King's gold for the Earl of Mar. The MacIntyres tried to look after him, but once he was fit and well they could not keep him any more. He rose one morning and left to look for the buried gold. However strong his sense of duty, however committed he was to the cause, however much he wanted to fulfil his mission, he simply could not. He could remember burying the gold and little else after it. He knew he had been in a fight that nearly killed him but all that remained of the incident were a few blurred impressions. All he knew was that he had to find the gold. But the damage to his memory was such that he could not remember where he had buried it. His companions had been either killed or transported and he was the only one left. He was a man obsessed, walking endlessly round the slopes of Ben Ledi and further afield, looking for anything that might remind him of where he had left the King's Gold. The local people became used to him on his travels and as he was clearly brain-damaged, all took turns to feed him and give him clothes when he needed them.

For many years after the '15 he was to be seen haunting the area, muttering constantly to himself, 'I must find the gold, the Earl needs it.' He was completely unaware that Bobbing John had long fled the country. The people in the area came to call him Duncan the Seeker and it was many years later that one of the sons of the MacIntyres who had looked after him, found his body lying in the heather on the hill. He had lost the gold but never his loyalty to the cause.

The Battle that Wasn't

THERE ARE MANY EXAMPLES of rather pathetic leadership skills amongst the Jacobites in 1715, but they were not alone. As it was still the norm in those days for aristocrats to advance to the most senior military ranks, with little or no regard for actual tactical or strategic skills, this is hardly very surprising. In October, General Alexander Gordon of Auchintool was sent to the west of Scotland by the Earl of Mar. He marched on Inverary, the chief seat of the Campbells in their Argyll homelands, with a force of 4,000 men. The Duke of Argyll's brother, Archibald Campbell, the Earl of Islay, was in charge of the forces loyal to the Hanoverians in the west, and he had fortified the town itself by digging trenches and had gathered in nearly 2,500 men, including regular troops and Campbell clansmen. His combined force was probably about 2,500 men, some of whom were cavalry.

Gordon made his camp a mile or so to the north-east of Inverary. Whether or not he was eager for battle is unclear. On the advice of the Jacobite Campbell of Glendaruel, he had come west hoping to gather a great number of new recruits from Argyll and the adjoining areas. Gordon's thinking was that if he could keep Islay and his troops cornered in Inverary, the chances of men coming to join him would be that much greater. Islay meanwhile, having found out that the Jacobite army was considerably larger than the number of troops at his command, was reluctant to sally forth and close with the enemy. So matters stood at a bit of a standstill for a few days, with neither side doing very much at all.

Following Campbell of Glendaruel's advice, Gordon decided to try and recruit more men. So a force of about 200 men was sent out under the leadership of Campbell of Glenlyon, another of his clan siding with the Stewarts. It was thought that a Campbell would have the best chance of attracting new men in the district of Lorn. However, it was Campbell country and the Duke of Islay soon got word of what was happening. To counteract this effort Islay sent out a troop of 700 clansmen under the leadership of one of the most experienced soldiers of his clan. This was Colonel Campbell of Fonab, who set off north to try and intercept Glenlyon. Right enough he came up with the Jacobite force near a wee village, or clachan, at the foot of Loch Nell, a few miles east of Oban. When the Jacobite forces saw the Hanoverian men approaching they drew themselves up in line of battle across the side of a small hill. Fonab's men drew up opposite them and it was immediately clear that the Jacobites were outnumbered at least three to one. Glenlyon was mulling over whether to fight or flee when he saw a horseman detach from the opposite ranks. Obviously this was to be an attempt at having a parley. Spurring his own horse he moved forward, recognising as he did so that his opposite number was Fonab.

The old soldier rode up to him and the pair of them stopped midway between the two forces.

'Well then Glenlyon, are you well?' said Fonab politely.

'I am indeed Fonab, are you keeping well yourself?' he replied, pleased to see the older man despite the situation.

'Och well this is a pretty pass we have come to,' Fonab went on, 'and I think it would be a great disaster if we were to see Campbell fighting Campbell this day.'

'I would agree with that,' replied Genlyon slowly, 'but what have you in mind?'

At that Fonab told his younger kinsman what he thought should happen. The two of them sat on horseback between their respective forces, then Genlyon turned and rode back to his men to tell them of what was proposed. Well, not just proposed, but proposed and accepted. In order to avoid the horror of the clansmen fighting their own kin, Fonab suggested that Glenlyon's men should hand over their arms, he could ask no less, and that he and his men would convoy them out of Argyll and then release them to return to their own army. Glenlyon, well aware that there were plenty of arms back with the main body of the army at Perth, saw the sense in this – he too had no wish to see Campbells spilling Campbell blood, so happily accepted the terms. Accordingly, Fonab's men accompanied the Breadalbane men to the edge of Argyll where they happily waved farewell to their cousins, who headed back to join the Jacobite army. On hearing of this from Fonab, the Earl of Islay was furious and loudly berated the old soldier in front of a group of other officers. It was precisely this sort of behaviour that led many of the Campbells at Inverary to decide that Islay was getting above himself and there was a consequent outbreak of desertion, amongst both officers and men. It would seem that the quality of leadership on both sides was clearly no match for the courage and commitment, and in this case the common sense, of the men under their command.

A few days later a more substantial force of Jacobites arrived in the area. Soon after, the Campbell troops in Inverary were wakened in the night by a great noise of thundering hooves. The immediate suspicion was that the Jacobites were attacking with cavalry and men quickly formed up around the castle with their arms, ready to repel the enemy. As they stood ready to fire, the hooves got louder and suddenly there in front of them was a herd of horses. Not one had a saddle, a bridle or a rider. This was the herd of horses brought by Campbells and MacEacherns from Kintyre to provide Islay with some cavalry. Ever since Roman times when the local tribe was known as the Epidii, or horse warriors, the Kintyre men had been famous for their skill with horses, the name MacEachern itself meaning son of the horse. In this case however, they had not looked after their stock well, and had left them on a poor bit of grazing close to the town. The herd, dissatisfied with their location, had simply decided to move and look for better grazing! While moving across the river to a better meadow something spooked them, setting off a bit of a stampede. With the rattling of drums and the shouting of the officers the horses speeded up and headed off westwards in the night. A report of the time said 'At last the whole was found only to be a plot among the Kintyre horse to desert not to the enemy, but to their own country; for "tis to be supposed, the horses, as well as their owners, were of very loyal principles.' This put an end to Islay's cavalry for the meantime and once the horses had gone, the majority of the men went back to sleep.

Later, the very same night, a sergeant was doing the rounds of the sentries at Inverary. The sergeant had spent some hours in a tavern in the town during the evening and was somewhat the worse for wear. As he approached one of the sentries in the dark the sentry called out, 'Who goes there? State the password.'

The sergeant, due to the amount of drink he had taken, had completely forgotten the password, and simply called out. 'It is Sergeant Dougal Campbell...'

He got no chance to say any more. The sentry was already nervous because of the earlier incident with the horses, and, not receiving the password, raised his musket and fired at the indistinct figure he could see and the sergeant threw himself to the ground.

Pandemonium broke out. Up in the castle, Islay heard the shot and called at once for the drummer to beat the call to arms. All around the town men grabbed their muskets and headed for the mustering point on the castle green. The drunken sergeant, sobering up quickly, realised what he had done, and to cover his tracks, gave a great shout, 'The rebels, the rebels are coming.' At once, several other sentries began firing in the general direction of where they thought the Jacobites were camped.

All the Campbells and government forces were assembled on the castle green, where the troops were ordered into the trenches adjoining the town, and ordered to start firing, platoon by platoon, in the direction of where they thought rebels were. No one had any doubt that there was night attack under way from the north-east. So volley after volley rang out, orders being shouted by the officers the majority of whom it seems had retired behind the thick walls of Inverary Castle! Up in the Jacobite camp everyone was awakened by the noise and looking towards the town they saw the flashes of the persistent firing. Gordon knew he had not ordered a night attack and took the firing to be a celebration of the arrival of reinforcements for the Hanoverian forces. In a clear case of deciding that discretion was the better part of valour he at once put an order round that his men were to march back east as soon as the dawn rose.

Eventually Islay realised that there was no returning fire and orders were given to his men to cease firing. Such was the tenseness of the situation that they all stood to arms through the hours of darkness. Come the dawn it was obvious that there had been no attempted assault by the Jacobites, and it was only a short while later that word came in that the forces of General Gordon were heading back east towards Perth.

Eilean Donan

ONE OF THE MOST beautiful sights in Scotland is the castle of Eilean Donan, situated where Loch Alsh and Loch Duich meet on the mainland, opposite the Isle of Skye. Probably the most photographed and painted castle in Britain, there is an air of romance abut Eilean Donan that attracts tourists by the busload. Probably named after an early saint, the island has had some sort of castle on it since the 13th century and was long in the possession of the Mackenzie clan, though its strategic location meant that it changed hands many times, usually as result of bloodshed, and eventually became a MacRae stronghold. The original castle had been blown up by the government in 1719, after a truly pathetic attempt at rebellion by the Jacobites which involved a tiny force of Spanish soldiers, all of whom were captured by the British Army. The current building is the result of a restoration in the early 20th century. The castle has a long and varied history and by the 18th century, was in the hands of the government. And thereby hangs a tale long told locally.

When the Earl of Mar raised his standard at Braemar and headed to Perth there were many throughout the Highlands who rallied to support him in his attempt to bring back the King over the Water, James VIII of Scotland and III of Britain, according to Jacobite belief. Given the strength of the British Navy, Eilean Donan, which could easily be supplied by sea, was a very valuable strategic asset for the Government.

Now its location on the island, reached by a causeway from the shore, meant that the castle was extremely hard to take and as long as the British Army troops kept their wits about them, they should have been able to retain possession of the castle. But, as happened more than a few times in the Jacobite period, the army found itself outwitted.

The local people, who were all pretty much of a Jacobite persuasion, had heard that the Earl of Mar was raising an army to try and bring back the rightful king and many men from the area went to join him. In traditional Highland style this was not just because of the loyalty to the cause of the House of Stewart. It was also a chance to go on a major raid, for raiding was in the heart of the Highland warriors. Inter-clan raiding had been going on since time immemorial and the opportunity for some economic advantage, presented by a possible raid as far as England, was an exciting prospect. However, those who stayed behind looked on the castle with a fair degree of resentment. It was not long after the inconclusive Battle of Sheriffmuir, close to Dunblane, in November 1715, that one of the locals, a MacRae, decided to act. He was a man who had a fair amount of land under cultivation and had made it his business to be on good terms with the commander of the castle, a British Army captain, sending him fresh butter and cheese and the odd barrel of *uisge beatha*, whisky, leading to further supplies being requested, for which of course he did receive payment. He was thus relatively welcome in the castle, though he made a point always to go alone.

Now being quite far north, the harvest was often much later than further south, and in 1715 it was particularly late. The whole year the weather had been a bit strange and spring had not come till late April, and it was only now in November that the crops were ready to be harvested. MacRae realised that this might just provide an opportunity to do something for the Jacobite cause.

He went to the castle one morning and asked to speak to the Commander. When the captain came down to meet him at the gate and the usual pleasantries had been exchanged MacRae got to the point.

'Well Sir,' he said, 'I have a bit of a problem. I suppose you know that quite a few of our young lads have got all hot and bothered and have headed off to join the business in the south.'

'Yes Mr MacRae,' came the reply, 'I am aware of that sad fact. The level of loyalty to the Government around here is frankly terrible, but,' he added quickly, 'you have shown yourself to be a loyal subject and great help to us here at the castle,'

'Well I do appreciate you're saying so, but,' and here McRae paused to look quizzically at the soldier. 'I was wondering if I might ask a favour of you and your men.'

'Ask away,' smiled the commander, 'and if it is in my power to help you, I shall.'

'Grand,' said MacRae, and went on, 'you see with so many men having gone off and the summer having come so late it is only now that my corn has ripened, and there are not enough men around to help me get it in. I fear the weather is about to break and if I can't get the crops in it will go hard with me and my family this winter. Would it be at all possible for you to loan me some men to help me get my harvest in?'

'Yes I think I could manage that,' said the captain, sure that he was dealing with a loyal subject. In essence what MacRae told him was true, a considerable number of local men had gone off to join the Earl of Mar, and they suffered extensively at the Battle of Sheriffmuir, as many as 60 MacRaes falling in the battle. However not all the local men had gone south, though according to MacRae they were all too busy trying to get their own harvests in to give him the help he needed.

So later that same day the captain and the majority of the garrison, with only a few of them carrying firearms, left the castle and went to help MacRae with his harvest, just a couple of miles down the Loch Duich. Behind them they had left only a handful of men.

And that handful of men soon had a surprise. As soon as the main body of troops had disappeared from sight around a bend in the road, a group of a dozen or so MacRaes started creeping through the water along the outside of the causeway.

Another half dozen had been lying close to the castle gate since before dawn, when they had swum out from the shore. At the gate were two soldiers. They never had a chance. Before they knew what was happening they were overpowered and the MacRaes rushed into the castle, it was over in minutes, without a shot being fired. A few hours later, after having got in MacRae's crops and having been rewarded with a liberal amount of the very best locally made whisky, the captain and his men came back to Eilean Donan. As they came to the causeway they saw the gate was closed and looking up saw their flag had been struck and the battlement was lined with armed Highlanders pointing their own muskets at them. They had no choice but to turn back. A direct assault would have been fatal. The captain was furious at this deception and he and his men, almost completely unarmed, hurried back to the farm they had just left, but there was no sign of MacRae. With few arms, no provisions and little hope of any, the captain and his men headed off towards Inverness, where they arrived hungry, bedraggled and embarrassed, several days later.

Borlum Bolts

AFTER THE DISASTER at Preston, when Thomas Forster, a Northumberland squire, had surrendered to the British Army on 14 November 1715, the leaders of the Jacobite force were transported to London for trial. Among them was MacIntosh of Borlum, who had shown his worth as a soldier in the crossing of the Firth of Forth under the noses of Royal Navy ships and marching south to join the English Jacobites. He, like his men, many of whom were of his own kin, had been outraged by Forster's surrender to the government troops. They had wanted to fight on and at the least they would have had a chance to fight their way clear of Preston and head back to Scotland. Forster's disgraceful cowardice had ensured that many of them were executed and large numbers of them were transported to the West Indies, never to see their beloved Highlands again. By this time Borlum was a man in his mid 50s but was still fit and strong. A tall, fair-haired man, he was intelligent and cultured but when it came to battle, he had a reputation of being as stubborn as a mule and as savage as a tiger. On being transported to Newgate prison in London he immediately began thinking about how to escape. As early as 11 April, one of the Jacobite prisoners had managed to escape. This was Thomas Forster himself who had made off using a duplicate key in the middle of a drinking session with the Governor of Newgate prison, Mr Pitt. This escape was so slickly organised and carried out that there were those who said that the government themselves were behind it. It seems the authorities were a little reluctant to publicly try a man who was both a Member of Parliament and a Protestant, for fear of the effect on public opinion. However Borlum, a well-liked and respected soldier, often referred to as the 'Old Brigadier,' didn't have to rely on the subtleties of a Nithsdale or secret government connivance to get out of Newgate.

Now during the day in the prison, the prisoners were generally free to wander round the courtyard that lay behind the great locked gates of the prison. One of the gates had a door in it to allow people in and out without always having to swing open the massive gates themselves, a manoeuvre that entailed clearing the courtyard of the prisoners. In the course of a normal day turnkeys, soldiers, members of the families of the non-political prisoners and a variety of trades-men came and went through this door. It was always guarded but sometimes by no more than a turnkey and a couple of soldiers. Beyond the gate lay the teeming streets of London, constantly thronged with people, carts and coaches.

On the evening of 4 May a large group of the Jacobite prisoners, numbering nearly 60, were dining together with a fair amount of wine and punch being consumed. They all seemed to be merry and remarkably happy considering their circumstances and the guards thought little of it when they gathered in the press-yard, the area behind the gate, supposedly to get some fresh air. Borlum however had more than fresh air on his mind and had already discussed possibilities with some of his compatriots, including his son and his brother, who had been captured with him at Preston, and the redoubtable Charles Wogan who had later rescued Princess Clementina Sobieska, Prince Charlie's mother-to-be from the Schloss Ambras in Austria. There were only a couple of turnkeys guarding the gate when MacIntosh shouted in Gaelic, 'Right lads, let's get at them!'

Before they could react the two turnkeys were overpowered by Borlum and half a dozen others. The keys were stripped from their belts, the door in the gate opened and the whole group of Jacobite prisoners streamed out into the street. Borlum and his helpers at the gate knew exactly where they were going. He had been in London on several occasions and knew his way around. Once they had reached the first corner they slowed down and walked calmly to a house owned by a Jacobite sympathiser, several streets away. Within a couple of days Borlum and his son travelled to Ipsden Bassett in Oxfordshire, where his sister lived with her husband, Thomas Reade, the local squire. Here they stayed till arrangements could be made for a passage to France. Sadly, Borlum's brother was later re-captured at Rochester and returned to Newgate.

As they had left the prison, the other Jacobites also saw their chance, quite a few of them having had too much wine or punch. Out they came and spread out through the streets around the prison. Many of them had no idea of where they were going and over the next couple of hours were rounded up by the soldiers who were summoned after the mass breakout. Some of them were found after having asked directions, their Scottish accents giving them away, while others were seen running away from the jail and noticed by the crowds in the street. A few others were simply too drunk to get far and missed their chance. Some, however, were given help and also got away. The fault lines between Hanoverian and Jacobite ran right through society and there were many who, if not actually on one side or the other, had definite leanings, and others who considered that a political difference with a friend was no reason to wish him imprisoned, executed or transported. In all. about a dozen of the prisoners managed to escape successfully at the same time as Old Borlum.

One of these was Robert Hepburn of Keith. Like many of his co-prisoners he had no idea that Borlum was going to try and break out, and there were those that said Borlum himself only decided at the last minute, but was happy to seize the opportunity. By the time he was in the street outside the prison, Borlum and his party had already disappeared and he just ran. A few minutes later he realised he was lost. He knew that his wife and family had come down to London and were living near the prison, but how could he find them in this warren of streets? If he asked any kind of directions he would show himself to be a Scot and behind him he could already hear the soldiers searching through the streets. As he walked briskly along, his heart thumping and his mind racing, he looked up at a house he was passing. At first he could not believe his eyes. There in the window was a large and ancient pewter plate that he had seen many times before. It was the Keith Tankard and had been in his family for generations! At once he hammered on the door of the house, and it was opened by none other than his wife! It was an emotional and tearful reunion. Once they had calmed down they sat down together and he learned that she had rented this house under a false name to be near to him. She had tried many times to get to see him but without success. Lying low for a couple of days, the Keith family then followed Borlum's example and found safety in France.

However, The escape from Newgate was not the end of the adventures of William MacIntosh of Borlum. While living in France he was active in Jacobite affairs and, like so many of his country-men, longed for the chance to return to Scotland and try again. In 1719 the chance did come again and Borlum landed at Stornoway in April, with the regiment of Spanish soldiers who had come to support another rising. This attempt at Jacobite rebellion was notable for even worse planning and leadership than the '15. After the utter ineptitude of the Jacobite command at the battle of Glen Shiel, the Spanish soldiers surrendered and when they were transported to Edinburgh Castle, Borlum was with them. Why he had not simply faded away into the Highlands in the chaos at the end of the battle is a mystery but perhaps his sense of honour prevented him from deserting the Spanish commander Don Nicolás Bolaño, in his hour of need.

Having given their parole, once they were in Edinburgh, the Spanish officers were given the liberty of the town, and after having had to rely on local Jacobite sympathisers for food and other necessities, they were returned to Spain in October. Parole, however, was not a privilege extended to Borlum. Having already escaped once and then having had the temerity to come out in the Jacobite cause he was tried, found guilty and sentenced to be imprisoned in Edinburgh Castle for life. In those times that meant life, he was to stay there till he died in 1743. However although his body was imprisoned his mind was not and during the long years of his imprisonment he wrote and had published several works on improve-ments in agriculture, a topic of consuming interest at the time. All who knew him spoke highly of William MacIntosh and the fact he was never released, when so many others were pardoned, even still suggests little more than venomous pique on the part of the British government.

A Great Escape

IN JULY 1718 JAMES STEWART, the Old Pretender as he was known to the Hanoverians, asked for the hand of Princess Clementina Sobieska in marriage. She was the grand-daughter of the Polish king, John III Sobieski, a man renowned for having seen off the Turkish siege of Vienna in 1683 and, in the eyes of many, saving Christian Europe from the infidels. The Polish Royal Family were of course Catholic and Sobieski himself must have been perfectly well aware of what he was doing when he gave his consent to the marriage. Now, James had never seen Clementina at this stage, a not unusual circumstance amongst royalty at the time. She had been recommended to him by Charles Wogan, one of his most trusted advisers, who had been touring Europe on his behalf looking for just such a suitable bride. Wogan was a prominent Jacobite, having been taken prisoner at Preston in 1715 then making his escape from Newgate prison along with MacIntosh of Borlum. Still only in his 20s, he had served for two years in Dillon's Regiment in the French army, and was a man of considerable talent and courage. Now when George I heard of the planned marriage he was furious. The last thing he wanted was the exiled Stewart, claimant to the throne, producing an heir! And the fact that by the standards of the time Clementina was a good catch only made things worse. For she would bring a considerable amount of money as well as the famous Sobieski jewels with her when she went to Rome to marry James. He was in a win-win situation and George was determined to stop the marriage happening, any way he could. His first step was to try to get the Austro-Hungarian Emperor, Charles VI, to put a stop to the marriage. Charles was not particularly keen to interfere in such matters but as he wanted to keep up good relations with the British crown, he rather reluctantly gave orders for the princess to be detained at Innsbruck. She was on her way to Rome when she was arrested and detained.

Both her father and her prospective husband immediately complained to Charles VI but he appeared to be adamant that the marriage should not happen. He had made up his mind and would not be swayed from it. At this point, the courage and commitment of the Stewarts and their followers came into play. James had no intention of being deprived of his bride, realising as he did that George was behind this. It was bad enough that the man was sitting on his throne but for him to try and stop his marriage was just too much. Wogan, having already shown his abilities, was just the man to be sent to rescue the princess. So it was that in November 1718 Wogan turned up in Innsbruck posing as a French merchant. Like many Irish and Scot Jacobites of the time, he was fluent in several European languages and knew his way about the continent.

When he got there he found that Clementina, and her mother, were being kept in some comfort in the great medieval castle known as the Schloss Ambras. This great fortress was to test Wogan's abilities to the full. Back in Rome, as the months passed and no word came back, James began to despair of ever seeing his bride, but progress in Innsbruck, if slow, was steady and the redoubtable Wogan was getting on with things. Once he had laid his plans, he contacted the princess and her party and informed them of what he intended doing. The plan involved using several people, so he left Innsbruck to collect together a group of trusted and capable Jacobite friends, still passing himself off as a Frenchman. It was this that slowed matters down.

In April of the following year he returned to Innsbruck with his small party. There was his uncle, Major Gaydon, Captains John Misset and Luke O'Toole from Dillon's regiment in the French army, and with them were Mrs Misset and her maid Janetta. Major and Mrs Misset were passed off as the Comte and Comtesse de Cernes and Janetta as their daughter, with Wogan posing as the Comte's brother and Misset and O'Toole acting as their servants. They took up residence in a high-class inn not far from the Schloss itself. The maid, Janetta, had only been told that the group were hoping to rescue a young heiress whose father was attempting to stop her marrying

Captain O'Toole, with whom she was deeply in love. Once everything had been arranged, Janetta was taken to the Schloss Ambras by Wogan. Here they were met by Kotski, one of Clementina's pages, who brought Janetta into the castle telling the guards that she was the mistress of the steward of the Schloss, Chateaudoux, a Frenchman, who was in on the plot. Wogan left the castle gate and took up a place in hiding nearby.

Clementina had been well briefed in advance by Kotski and that evening she had complained of feeling unwell and had retired to her bedroom, saying that if the cold misty weather did not improve she was going to stay in her bed the following day as well. Her guards accepted this at face value and she went to her private room, after all she was a princess and they were used to obeying orders. Once there, she sat and wrote a letter to Charles VI. This was to explain that what she was doing was her own idea and that her mother had no part in the proceedings. Once she had written and sealed the letter, she wasted no time in packing up her famous jewels and putting on a heavy fur-lined cloak. She then sat waiting. She did not have long to wait. Chateaudoux and Janetta were shown into her room by Kotski, Janetta immediately went into the princess's bed – the Emperor's men had instructions to check on her at least twice a day – and Clementina went into the room where her mother was.

'Mother, I am going now to meet my intended husband. The maid that will take my place has arrived and before I go I want you to give me your blessing,' she said.

At this, both of them became rather emotional and there were hugs and kisses before the princess went on her way. Outside, Wogan's plans were unfolding nicely. Kotski went down to the front gate of the Schloss with the princess wearing Janetta's cloak over her own. Janetta was a bit bigger and taller than Clementina but before arriving she had put on low-heeled shoes and with Clementina wearing stylish high-heeled shoes the two were about the same height. With the princess wearing two cloaks the deception passed off without a problem. Once they were through the gates of the Schloss, Wogan came forward from where he had been hiding and the three of them scurried off to the nearby inn where the others were waiting, Kotski carrying the parcelled up Sobieski jewels. As soon as they were at the inn Clementina thanked Kotski profusely, and he headed back to the Schloss to try and make things seem as normal as possible. Then Mrs Missett helped Clementina change into travelling clothes and the group headed off towards the border between Austria and the northern Italian republic of St Mark.

They were congratulating themselves that everything had gone like clockwork when Clementina realised something was missing. She lad left the case of jewels back at the inn! Somebody would have to go back for them. At that point Captain O'Toole said he would do it and while the others waited freezing in the cold alpine night, the Irishman rode back at breakneck speed to Innsbruck. It was late at night when he got there and the inn was dark. O'Toole was reluctant to knock up the staff at the inn and alert them to the fact that his party had gone off in the night. He was a man of some considerable strength and he simply lifted the front door of the inn off its hinges and made his way silently into the building. He had no intention of striking a light and in the darkness he gently felt his way to the room they had been in. Once he was in he groped about in the dark till he found the valuable parcel. At once he made his way back to the open door, leapt on his horse and took off southwards.

His companions were growing increasingly restive. They were all beginning to imagine that the escape had been discovered and that O'Toole and the jewels had been captured when they heard the sound of hoof-beats. They all looked at each other, hearts in their mouths. Had the alarm been raised and a company of guards sent to capture them?

'Och no it's only the one horse,' said Wogan with relief, 'it'll be O'Toole himself.'

Within seconds, the truth of the statement was made plain and once they had congratulated O'Toole, the small group of Jacobites headed off on their way. However, they were not yet home and dry, for they still had many miles of the Austrian Tyrol to cross before they were safe beyond the border.

Back at Schloss Ambras, the deception went well enough the following day, but by the next day the Emperor's guards were becoming a little suspicious as the princess was still in bed and no doctor had been called. At that, Kotski got Janetta out of the bed and showed her a tiny, damp and miserable little hole in the wall just outside the princess' apartments, into which she squeezed herself. The game was then up, for the next time the guards arrived it was clear to them that the princess had escaped. The castle was searched but Janetta wasn't found. Poor Kotski, however, fell under suspicion and ran off through the streets of Innsbruck before he was captured and dragged back to the castle. Here, Clementina's mother produced her daughter's letter and the upshot of it was that she was absolved of any blame. On hearing of the dramatic escape, Charles VI realised that he could hedge his bets, after all the Jacobite cause might yet prove successful, and it certainly appears that he didn't pursue the fugitives with as much rigour as he might have.

However one agent, who it seems was probably in the pay of the British government, did set off after the fleeing group and he arrived at the inn they were staying at, the night before they intended crossing the border from Austria. O'Toole again stepped into the breach! He recognised the man from Innsbruck and struck up a conversation with him in the inn. He ordered up a bottle of wine and then another. Unknown to his companion, however, the wine, arriving in jugs, had been spiked with brandy by Mrs Missett, and by the end of the second bottle the man was so hopelessly drunk he was legless and Wogan was able to lead the party off to the border and safety with no further problems.

After all this adventure it would be fitting to say that the intended couple soon met and fell in love at first sight. In fact, James was in Spain by the time Clementina arrived in Rome. As ever he was attempting to drum up support for his claim to the British throne. This meant that the much longed for marriage was eventually carried out by proxy in Bologna, with Murray of Broughton standing in for James. The marriage had to wait four months before being consummated. Clementina spent the time living with the Ursuline Nuns as a guest of the Pope. Eventually James returned, landing on the Italian coast at Livorno on 27 August, and meeting his bride a few days later at Montefiascone, on 1 September. Here the real wedding took place, blessed by the local bishop on direct orders from the Pope. As for George 1, he made his feelings clear in a letter to the Emperor in which he expressed his displeasure and demand that he punish the Sobieskis. Much good it did him! Charles vi thought it better to let things lie as they were, and the Jacobite cause had a romantic and dramatic story to tell around the courts of Europe, which did their cause no harm at all.

A Dangerous Jacobite

IN THE YEARS BETWEEN the risings of 1715 and 1745 there was a great deal of Jacobite plotting going on. Much of it, no doubt, consisted of little more than bravado in taverns, even while more serious plans were being laid. One of the most common manifestations of support for the Jacobite cause was the surreptitious toast to the 'King over the Water'. This could be accomplished in the midst of a normal conversation simply by passing the right hand over one's glass, a simple sign understood by all Jacobite supporters and many of those who simply played at it. For amongst the less privileged ranks of contemporary society, as in many human societies at many times, there was a strong tendency to support anyone other than whoever was currently in power, particularly if there was some chance those currently holding power would be humbled. Such behaviour greatly distressed some of the more devout Protestants in the capital, some of whom were very much in the habit of following the tenets of their covenanting forebears. One of these was a strict adherence to Sabbatarianism, the idea that the only acceptable activities on Sundays were those that involved contemplation and prayer. A group of such Puritans lived together in the closes around the West Bow, just off the Grassmarket in the 1730s. Such was their excessive piety that they were known about Edinburgh as the Bowhead Saints. As is usual with over-pious people, they were not known for their sense of humour and believed that everyone should do as they did. Even at this late date there were still citizen's patrols walking the streets during divine service on a Sunday, on the look-out for those who they considered to be breaking the Sabbath. The wiser heads simply kept out of sight during the various hours of a Sunday that these patrols were about. Various events were talked of, like the time when they came upon a joint of meat being roasted over an open fire in the back vennel of one of the closes. Such blatant Sabbath breaking was not to be tolerated and the patrol duly confiscated the meat from off its spit leaving its owner and his family hungry. However, as they themselves had no hand in its cooking, it was said they saw the provision of a succulent feast as divine providence and had no hesitation in devouring it themselves. Such were the practicalities of their Christian commitment.

However, on another occasion they actually took themselves a prisoner and one which, truth be told, caused them some problems. It was the custom amongst many people of the time, no matter their political affiliation, to buy songbirds and teach them the current songs of their own party, Jacobites as well as Whigs. One Saturday evening a staunch Jacobite had left his blackbird in its cage outside a window in his tenement close, possibly because he was more concerned with singing songs himself as result of a glass or two of claret. Anyway, come the morning the bird happily began trilling away its limited repertoire of tunes, all of which were clearly anti-Hanoverian. Its owner lay in his bed oblivious of what was going on as the hour of the first Sunday service approached. Never a devout man, he was unconcerned that he might miss going to church at all. And so it came to pass that the devout band of brothers scouring the streets for sinners came past his window. To their shock and horror they heard the bird as they approached giving forth the scandalous and treasonous tune, *The King shall come into his own again.* The place where its cage was attached to the wall was accessible to several apartments and they were at a loss as to who should carry the blame for this disgraceful affair.

As always with such groups, there was one who felt the affront so badly he felt he must do something. Accordingly he got his companions to fetch a ladder, up which he climbed, and removed the bird in its cage from the wall. Coming down with the bird he looked at his companions, all of whom were a little quizzical as to what he intended doing now. But such men are always ready to rise to any occasion and he said, with something of an air of solemnity.

'Right we shall just lock this foul creature up in the guard room.'

Whether he hoped a spell in the clink would make the bird mend its ways is unclear. The man's pomposity gave rise to verse by

Pennycook, a local rhymester, who put these words in the poor man's mouth

> 'Had ye been taught by me, a Bowhead saint
> You'd sung the Solemn League and Covenant
> Bessy of Lanark, or the Last Good-Night
> But you're a bird prelatic – that's not right
> Oh could my baton reach those laverock too
> They're chanting Jamie, Jamie just like you
> I hate vain birds who lead malignant lives
> But love the chanters to the Bowhead wives'

This soon became popular in those taverns where the silent toast to the King over the Water were the norm and many were taken by the notion that even the larks were singing of the return of the Stewarts. What the Bowhead saints said when confronted with the lines, as they must have been, has not come down to us.

Highland Courtesy

COCKADES WERE DECORATIVE RIBBONS affixed to hats, and the Jacobites of the '45 adopted white ones as a sign of their loyalty to the Stewart cause. Given that most of the Jacobite Army were irregular troops, and that uniforms were a rarity, they served as a useful identification, in battle as well as on the streets of Scotland's towns, once the campaign was underway. There have been those who have said that the reason the white cockade was chosen was because Prince Charlie picked a white rose and stuck it in his own bonnet, a story that is thought to have inspired the Robert Burns song 'My Love was born in Aberdeen.' However, as different-coloured cockades or hat decorations had been used as a sign of political and military allegiances since the 17th century, this is hardly likely. It is an example of the kind of story, and song, that came into being in the late 18th and early 19th centuries, as the horrors of Culloden faded from public consciousness and the fear of resurgent Jacobitism was overtaken by a romantic view of Scotland's past, popularised by Sir Walter Scott and others. That said, chivalry was not unknown amongst the Jacobites.

During the sojourn of the Highland army in England in November 1745, a party of MacDonalds approached Rose Castle near Carlisle, which was then occupied by a man called Dacre, from Cumberland. The Highlanders came to the castle doors, fully armed, and demanded to be quartered there in such a way as to make it clear that they had no intention of being refused. The servant who answered the door was no coward and refused to be intimated.

'I'm afraid, Sir,' he said calmly to Donald MacDonald of Kinlochmoidart, who was leading the contingent, 'that it is a most inconvenient time.'

'Whatever do you mean?' demanded MacDonald, a bit taken aback at the man's coolness and bravery.

'Well, Sir, the lady of the house, Mrs Dacre, has just given birth to a fine young daughter, and, as you can imagine, we are all at sixes and sevens,' the man replied.

'God forbid that I or any of my kin here should give the lady any further inconvenience at such a time,' MacDonald said and, turning to his companions, he addressed them briefly in Gaelic.

Most of the contingent turned as if to go when a thought crossed MacDonald's mind. Perhaps this was just a clever ploy. Calling to his kinsmen to wait for a few minutes, he turned back to the man standing at the castle door.

'Would you think it possible that your mistress would let me see the infant,' he asked in a polite but decisive manner. The servant was left in no doubt that this was no request but an order, and, given the presence of so many heavily armed Highlanders, an order that would have to be obeyed.

'I can see no harm in that at all,' said the servant, as calm as you like. 'If you will just wait here a minute, Sir, I shall see if I can fetch the child.'

He turned and went back inside only to reappear a few minutes later accompanied by a young maid, who was carrying the new-born infant warmly wrapped in a blanket. She brought the infant to MacDonald and held her up for him to see.

Looking down on the infant with a smile, the fierce-looking Highland warrior took his bonnet from his head. Then, unpinning the white cockade from the bonnet he pinned it to the front of the blanket the newborn babe was wrapped in.

'There,' he said with a gentle smile. 'That will be a token to any of our comrades who come this way that Donald MacDonald of Kinlochmoidart has taken the family of Castle Rose under his protection.'

He then turned to the servant and, looking beyond him into to the castle itself, saw a man standing in the shadows beyond the door. He called for the man to come forward. It was the child's father and, after congratulating him on the birth of his daughter, Donald shook the clearly terrified man by the hand and said, 'You will not be bothered further by any of our troops and may the child be healthy and happy all her days.'

He then turned and said a few more words to his men at which point the entire contingent departed.

As for the white cockade, it became a treasured possession in the Dacre family and was particularly appreciated by Mary Dacre, who was the baby brought to the door. Throughout her childhood she repeatedly asked to be told the story of what had happened when the Highlanders arrived on the day of her birth. When she grew up, she married and became Lady Clerk of Penicuik and every year on her birthday she took great pleasure in wearing the white cockade in remembrance of the gallant Highland chief who had called at Rose Castle in 1745.

As for Donald, he paid the ultimate price for his loyalty to the Jacobite cause.

First Impressions

IN JULY 1746, the red-coated army of the British government was sweeping through the Highlands trying to root out rebels. There was widespread brutality, rape and murder. Much of it was carried out by Scots loyal to the government, or in some cases, those simply looking for their revenge on traditional enemies. Stewart Shaw of Inch-Croy just north of Culloden Moor, had been out with the Mackintoshes in support of the Prince and had gone into hiding after the battle. His wife and three daughters were left helpless at Inch-Croy. Times were hard especially living so close to the battle-field but they were lucky and had been spared the vicious excesses of the Hanoverian troops during the battle, and in the weeks after-wards. One day that July however, a tall, powerful, red-headed Highlander came to their door claiming to be one Sergeant Campbell, sent to search the house for the rebel Shaw. He was fully armed with sword and pistols and had a targe slung across his back.

Mrs Shaw, like so many Scots women down the centuries was a woman of spirit and said, 'I would far rather a dozen of the Government's Hessian mercenaries tramped through my house than one such as you, a Campbell and a traitor to his own king and people.'

'Och well, Mrs Shaw,' the man replied with a crooked smile, 'that's as may be but I am thinking you will fare better at the hands of one of your own countrymen than at the hands of the Germans, or even the English soldiers. Now will you be giving me the keys to the house or not?'

Mrs Shaw was all too aware that there was little she and her daughters could do against this big Campbell, armed as he was. So she disdainfully flung the keys to the house at his feet. Picking them up, he began to search the house methodically, stopping regularly to look out of various windows, whilst Mrs Shaw kept up a barrage of insults, to which he paid not the slightest attention. At last he came to main bedroom and was looking behind a large wardrobe he had pulled away from the wall when there was the sound of horses outside. At once, he turned and looked at the lady of the house, pointed silently at the head of her bed with his left hand and put the first finger of his right hand to his lips. She gazed at him in amazement as the sound of heavy boot-clad feet thundered up the stairs.

The door swung open and in came a red-coated officer with five dragoons, behind him in the doorway, all with sword or a pistol in hand.

'Right now, what's going on here?' demanded the officer, his eyes swinging between Mrs Shaw and the big Highlander.

'I am so glad you are here sir,' blustered Mrs Shaw. 'This coarse ruffian of a sergeant has been turning everything topsy-turvy searching the house. There is no one here but my daughters and I, and he refuses to accept it.'

The officer glared at the kilted man. 'Is that so? Right you brute, be off with you. If there are any rebels here, I'll be answerable for them. Get out!' he spat at the kilted figure before him.

'Och no, I don't think so,' replied the Highlander, his right hand on the pistol in his belt. 'I have been commissioned to search the place and I was here before you. I have been issued with orders from head-quarters and any reward coming is to be mine. You and your men can go.'

'What, you Scotch mongrel?' shouted the officer, going red in the face at this effrontery, 'Show me your commission this instant.'

'Och I think you should be showing me your commission first if you are demanding mine,' replied the other in a calm and steady voice.

'I am Cornet Letham of Cobham's dragoons and have no need to show the likes of you anything. Now, who exactly is your commanding officer?' came the riposte.

'Well,' said the Highlander with a grim smile, 'I think I can say that I am under the orders of a better gentleman than yourself, or any that have ever commanded you.'

'What?' shouted Letham, 'What did you say? One better than anyone who has ever commanded me? How dare you! That is treason and you, sir, are clearly a damned rebel and I arrest you as such here and now.'

So saying, he came forward and, sure in the knowledge that he had five armed men at his back, he tried to grab him by the throat. He had misread his opponent. The tall Highlander whipped out his pistol, swung back his right arm and gave the officer a thunderbolt of a blow to the side of his head with the butt of the weapon. As the officer fell senseless to the floor, his men levelled their pistols at the red headed man but, with remarkable speed, he leapt behind the wardrobe, drawing his other pistol as he moved. Now without a clear shot, the dragoons were in a bit of a fix. The doorway to the room was narrow and only one man at a time could come through it. That man would be an easy target for the Highlander, protected as he was by the solid wood of the press. It was a stand-off.

After a whispered conversation two of the dragoons went out of the house. Their plan was to get at their enemy through the small window in the room. As soon as they smashed the glass in the window, they were sure they would soon have him at their mercy. They couldn't see him behind the press but if he moved they would shoot him down and their friends could then come safely into the room.

Realising their plan the Highlander had replaced his pistols in his belt and, with his left hand he took out his dirk, that vicious and most useful weapon and tool of the Highland warrior. Then he took his blue bonnet and put it over the handle of his dirk and just showed the edge of it round the corner of the heavy press as he unsheathed his sword with his right hand. At once, both dragoons at the window, keen to get in a fatal shot, let fire. As the bullets tore through his bonnet, the Highlander leapt out from his position and out through the doorway, swinging his sword in one hand and his dirk in the other. He came at the soldiers in the doorway so fast they had no time to fire their pistols, and the sight of the whirling steel terrified them. They were veterans, and realised that in the enclosed space the sweeping blades of the big Highlander would be fatal. They ran for the door tugging at their swords. They thought that once outside, they would soon cut him down. But they never had a chance. In their heavy coats and great boots they were no match for the man bearing down on them and two of them were chopped down before they even reached the front door. The third man looked over his shoulder to see his companions fall as he ran off down the road. He hadn't gone more than few yards before he too was cut down. The other two, who had been at the window, came round the corner of the house to see their comrade fall and made for their horses.

The red headed Highlander saw them and, as they mounted and took off, he leapt on Letham's horse and chased after them, shouting on them to turn and fight. The chase was witnessed by a couple of local lads, Peter Grant and Alexander McEachan, who were hiding out in the heather above the house. Often in later years they told of the Highlander flailing at his horse with the flat of his sword trying to catch up with the two Redcoats. He might have been a great fighter but as a horseman he was no match for the dragoons. In his efforts to catch up with them, he eventually rode into a boggy bit of ground and was thrown by the horse. Picking himself up, he looked after the fleeing soldiers then turned back to Inch-Croy. By the time he was nearing the house the two observers had run down from the hill and were waiting for him by the door of the house. 'Well done,' said McEachan with a smile as he held out his hand, 'that was a grand chase. Pity you didn't catch up with them though, Colonel.'

'Aye, right enough,' came the reply as the red headed man took McEachan's hand. He had recognised the two of them as men who had loyally followed his command throughout the abortive campaign to England and back. At this point, Mrs Shaw and her daughters came out from the outbuilding they had run to for shelter when the trouble had started.

'So you are no Campbell, after all then,' she said sternly.

'Colonel John Roy Stewart at your service,' he said, doffing his bullet-torn bonnet from off his head in a sweeping bow.

Mrs Shaw was much relieved. Her heart had almost stopped when

Stewart had pointed at the head of the bed just as the troops had arrived. They now went in and moved the bed to reveal a concealed door, behind which was a hidden room. In the cramped and window-less room, along with Shaw himself was Captain Finlayson and MacDonald of Lochgarry, who had heard all the noise but as they had no way of seeing what was happening, thought it better to stay where they were. All were glad to shake hands with their rescuer.

'But why for heaven's sake did you tell me you were a Campbell?' asked Mrs Shaw.

'Well,' replied Stewart, 'I had seen the dragoons coming and as long as you thought I was one of those damned Hanoverians I had a chance of getting the better of them. I didn't fancy taking on six men without some kind of delay. If you hadn't said I was one of them it was likely they would have shot me down as soon as they came into the house. I am sorry for having to deceive you though ma'am.'

'I am more than glad that you did, sir,' she said, 'for you have certainly done well by us all this day. But you had better all be off quick for those dragoons will be back with a great many of their accomplices before too long.'

And so it was that the six Jacobites headed off from Inch-Croy, Shaw himself unsure of when, or even if, he would see his home, his beloved wife and his lovely daughters again. He, Finlayson, MacEachan and Grant successfully made their way with the help of friends, through the Highlands to Glasgow where they managed to get aboard foreign ships and escape. Colonel Stewart and Lochgarry went west to join the Prince before they too left their beloved Scotland for France.

As for Mrs Shaw and her daughters, well they had a hard time of it when Cumberland heard that a single Highlander had bested six of his troops, killing four of them in the process. He made sure that Inch Croy was looted and burned, all the stock slaughtered and that the family of Shaw were locked up in prison for many months. But they never did manage to catch Colonel Stewart!

A Cross-Dressing Highlander

DONALD MACLAREN OF Wester Invernentie in Balquhidder was a captain in the Appin Regiment of the Jacobite Army in the '45. The regiment was composed mainly of Stewarts and MacLarens, with a sprinkling of McColls and other small septs. Under the leadership of Charles Stewart of Ardshiel, the Appin regiment had a significant role in the defeat of General Cope at Prestonpans in September 1745. They went with the Jacobite Army into England, were on the long retreat to Scotland and at the defeat at Culloden. During this overwhelming defeat for the Jacobite cause, seventeen men sacrificed themselves in protecting the standard of the Stewart clan before one of the regiment, Donald Livingston, cut the flag from its staff and carried it away.

Although Donald MacLaren was injured in the battle, he managed to get away from the battlefield, unlike so many of his countrymen who were executed in cold blood as they lay wounded. This was on the direct orders of the Duke of Cumberland. Despite his wounds, Donald managed to make his way south through the mountains to his native Balquhidder, where he hid in the hills to the north of Ben Ledi while slowly recovering from his injuries. In this period, virtually every glen in Scotland, outside of the Campbell heartland of Argyll and the lands north of Inverness, was garrisoned by Redcoat troops. So were many villages and towns throughout the whole country, including Aberdeen, Dundee and Stirling. The government was taking no chances on the rebellion bursting out again and almost all of Scotland was under direct military rule until well into the 1750s.

As well as the garrisons in the glens there were riding troops of dragoons regularly patrolling the passes through the Highlands. The official line was that this was to stop cattle-raiding, a long-established Highland tradition, but in fact it was part of a policy of not only keeping a lid on the Highlands but destroying the ancient clan system which kept thousands of armed men in a state of almost constant readiness for battle.

The long-term pacification of the Highlands, which Scottish monarchs had been trying to implement for centuries, was at last a viable project. It also meant that fugitive Jacobites, even with the support of the local population, had to be careful, very careful, not to be caught. One day, in the spring of 1747, Donald was just not careful enough. He was on the Braes of Leny overlooking the road to Loch Lubnaig when he was spotted by a patrol. As he was wearing Highland dress and carrying weapons, both of which were of course banned by the Disarming Act of 1746, the troops immediately chased him. They caught up with him and, after a short fight in which he was badly wounded, he was disarmed and made prisoner. This time, his recuperation was to take place in the confines of a cell in the nearby market town of Crieff, rather than in the clear, fresh air of his beloved hills. He was of course thoroughly searched after being captured but the searchers missed a *sgian dubh*, the small dark knife of the Highlander, in one of the folds of his plaid. Perhaps the fact that they had already found two of these knives in his clothing meant they missed this third one.

Donald was kept prisoner at Crieff till he was fit enough to travel and then was to be sent to Carlisle, where many of his fellow Jacobites had already been through the so-called judicial process of the time. It was a foregone conclusion that he would be found guilty of treason, the only question was whether he would be executed or transported to the West Indies to work as a slave in the blistering sun. Trying the rebels in England meant that they could be sentenced under English law without acknowledging the differences between English and Scots law, which for instance had no discretion to sentence anyone to transportation. Also English juries were thought reliable, while Scottish juries certainly were not! They couldn't be trusted to deliver the verdicts the government wanted. Now Donald was well aware of what was about to happen – all of Scotland knew what happened to Jacobites taken to Carlisle – and he had been thinking about how best to escape while he was regaining his strength in the cell. Although by the time he was to be taken to Carlisle his wound had almost healed completely, he made a show of still being very weak, and was apparently falling asleep at all times of the day.

It was therefore decided that he should be taken off to Carlisle on horseback, tied to the dragoon sitting in front of him. The rest of the party was made up of a dozen prisoners, the same number of soldiers and another five dragoons. From almost the moment they left Crieff, Donald made a great show of constantly nodding his head and falling onto the shoulder of the dragoon as if asleep. It didn't take long for the dragoon to stop nudging him to keep him awake and let him lie slumped against his back. This carried on through the first few days of the journey, and all the time Donald was keeping an eye open for an opportunity to make his move.

At last, after several days of travelling, and already a fair distance from the Highlands, he realised his chance was about to come. It was a cold and misty afternoon and the troop of soldiers and prisoners was heading towards Moffat through the Southern Uplands, close to the route of what is now the A701. Donald had been this way before on his return from Derby and remembered the lie of the land. He and the dragoon were bringing up the rear of the straggling column. In those days, the road ran along the top of the Devil's Beef Tub, a deep cauldron-like hollow in the hills, through which runs a brisk stream flowing into the River Annan. Trying his best to stay relaxed till the last possible second, Donald pretended to be asleep, slumped against the dragoon's back and waited till they were directly above the stream rolling and tumbling down the steep slope of the Beef Tub. Then, in an instant he slipped out his *sgian dubh*, cut through the rope tying him to the dragoon and leapt from the horse and rolled down the slope into the stream. He was gone in a flash and the dragoon gave out a yell to alert his comrades as he pulled up his horse and turned to see little more than a flash of tartan as Donald rolled down the slope and into the mist. The troops halted and the prisoners were lined up with levelled muskets pointed at them, as the dragoons dismounted to climb down after the escapee. By the time they were coming down the hillside, hampered a bit by their heavy boots, Donald had made his way to a boggy pool near the bottom of the hollow. Here he stood up to his neck in the water close by the bank, and using his trusty *sgian dubh* cut a large slice of turf, which he placed on his head. He could see little of the bank opposite but from any more than a foot or two away he was invisible. For almost an hour he stood there in the chill water as the dragoons passed back and forward, slashing at the tussocks of grass with their swords and cursing more and more.

At last, at a command from their officer, the dragoons gave up and headed back up to convoy the rest of their prisoners on their miserable journey. Giving them a good while longer to ensure no one had stayed behind, Donald at last hauled himself out of the water. He was chilled to the bone but wringing out his plaid he wrapped it about his body and climbed out of the Devil's Beef Tub and up the slopes of Clyde Law, heading north. The story of his daring escape from horseback soon spread around the area and for a long time after, the locals referred to the spot where he made his escape as MacLaurin's Leap.

His luck was in that day, for within a couple of hours he came across the carcass of a sheep that had recently fallen from a crag above. He sliced up as much of the beast as he could carry and stashed it inside his plaid. He knew better than to light a fire but the raw lamb, sliced thinly to aid chewing, would keep him going till he managed to get closer to home. Carefully keeping to cover wherever possible and making sure he would never show clearly against the skyline, Donald slowly moved north, regularly stopping to look around and using all the skills he had learned in the hills of his native Balquhidder to avoid being seen. Through the hills he went and passed the great fire hill of Tinto near Biggar, and on over the bleak moors to the west of the Pentland Hills. As he got closer to Stirling, he travelled only by night and at last he managed to pass Stirling and head up the Forth toward the Fords of Frew. Here, he crossed over the ancient ford and headed towards Callander, though by now his stock of food was gone. This did not bother him, he was close to home and knew where he could find friends he could trust. It was only a matter of another day or two before he was back on the Braes of Balquhidder, and he had no intention of leaving again. Between being out fighting in the Jacobite Army and then being in prison he had had enough of adventure. Now he only wanted to spend the rest of his life peacefully in the area he had been raised in.

There is an old cliché about the burnt child fearing the fire and Donald MacLaren was all too aware that he would have to be careful from now on. In fact, the Highlands were garrisoned for nearly another decade. The idea of permanently hiding out in the hills held little appeal and Donald, clearly a man of some intelligence, decided on another approach. He was fair-haired, slim and not too tall and as he had never had to shave more than once every few days, he decided he could turn his appearance to his advantage. So it was that the stock of bonny Highland lassies on the Braes of Balquhidder was increased by one. Well not that bonny, for though Donald could pass for a woman, even from quite close up, there was little chance that he would be taken for a beauty. So for the next year, taking care to keep out of the way of passing Redcoats whenever possible, Donald lived as a woman with some of his female cousins. Whenever he had to go anywhere other than the clachan they all lived in, or if there were Redcoats or strangers about, he would pull his shawl over his head, and try to walk as much like his cousins as he could. Not once was he stopped and questioned. It was a great relief for him though when the General Indemnity was passed later that same year and he could get out of wearing a woman's skirt and back into his kilt!

Gold in the Great Chanter

ALL ARMIES NEEDED MONEY, and the Jacobites in 1745 were no exception. Casks of gold were sent from France on a few occasions but not all of it was spent. On the west coast of Sutherland there was a large gully known as *Am Feodan Mor* – the Great Chanter – with a story of hidden Jacobite gold. The tale goes that one Duncan Macrae was given the care of a hogshead of gold to look after. Now a hogshead was a wooden barrel that held 72 gallons of liquid, so the amount of gold must have been considerable. Duncan was a man known to have the second-sight but he was also possessed of other powers. It was well-known in the Highlands that not only women had the power of magic, and in truth Duncan was thought of as being a bit of a wizard or magician. This made him the ideal man to hide the gold that might well be needed to feed, arm and pay for soldiers, if and when the prince returned to Scotland. So he and a couple of companions carried the gold to *Am Feodan Mor* and there it was buried with all the necessary spells and incantations that Duncan knew. They then left it hidden, sure that no one would ever find it unless they knew the secret of Duncan's spell. And a strange spell it was, for the hogshead could only be seen once every seven years on the very day that it had been buried. The secret was told only to a few but, as the years passed, and Prince Charles did not return to the Scottish Highlands, the secret was itself lost. This had a lot to do with the way the clanspeople were driven from their homes in the Highlands in the years after Culloden and, sporadically, ever since. Those leaving who knew the secret were never to return, and if Duncan Macrae and Prince Charlie's gold was ever mentioned among those who stayed, it was, well, 'just a story, wasn't it?'

Now, the area where the gold had been buried was deserted in 1746, but by the time a hundred years had passed, a *tigh dubh* or black house, had been built at the top of the gully where a croft had been carved out of the rough moorland. Many of the people from more fertile parts of the Highlands had been driven to farm and fish along the shores as the Clearances developed and sheep and deer took over the glens and straths.

There at the top of the gully, one fine summer's evening in 1844, 98 years to the day after the gold had been buried, the goodwife of the croft was sitting at her door spinning wool. She was spinning away, gently crooning an old lullaby when she looked down the slope and there, jutting from the ground, was the top of a wooden cask. She looked at it puzzled, for a moment. Then all at once she remembered the story her great-grandmother had told her of Duncan MacRae and Prince Charlie's gold, when she was just a few years old. Prince Charlie had never come back and the gold would belong to whoever found it – once the government took its cut of course. Realising that she could never get the gold out of the ground herself, she wondered what to do, as her man was off fishing at the time and wouldn't be back for some time. If she couldn't get it out of the ground before nightfall, it would disappear for another seven years!

Then it came to her what she had to do. There was plenty gold there for more than just her, her man and her three wee toddlers. She could well afford to go and seek help to get the great barrel out of the ground. Clambering down to where the barrel jutted from the earth with her distaff, she stuck it in the ground alongside the hogshead of gold, marking its position. Scrambling back up the slope, she dressed her children in their best clothes, picked up the littlest one, and the three of them headed off to the nearest village, about five miles off, to get help. By the time she reached the village, the gloaming was well advanced and it was clear that there was no way of getting aback to *Am Feodan Mor* before nightfall. So she sat up late that night with her relatives in the village, all excited about the discovery of the gold. Many glasses of peatreek, locally made whisky on which no duty would ever be paid, were drunk to toast Prince Charlie and his treasure and to the goodwife for her presence of mind in marking the gold's location before it disappeared again. There was many a bleary eye the following morning when a large group of villagers accompanied her back to the croft.

As they approached the rim of the great gorge hearts were a-fluttering with excitement – truth to tell there was no one there who didn't have a hard time of it and the thought of all the riches to some cleared many heads! They came to the croft house and passed it. As they all stood along the lip of the chasm and looked down it was obvious to them all just what had happened. For there was no sign at all of where the good wife had planted her distaff. Such was the power of Duncan MacRae's spell that when it had returned to hide the hogshead once more it also hid the distaff. Try as they might, not one of them could find a thing and it was a sad and tired crowd of villagers who returned home that day. As for the good wife, by the time the next seven years had passed she had half-a-dozen bairns to tend to, and she and her husband had moved off to one of the cities in the south of the country. Not everybody has forgotten all about Prince Charlie's gold though, and if only you knew the day that it re-appears you might just find it yourself.

The Silver Buttons

IT WAS 1746 AND Willie Mearns was 12 years old. He lived with his mother and two little sisters at Brocklas in Glen Clova, a two-roomed stone-built house overlooking a steep descent to the river South Esk. The year before he had stood at the Milton of Clova at the head of the glen and watched his father march off with the 800 men raised by David Ogilvy to join the Jacobite Army. A few months later the dreadful news of his father's death at Prestonpans had arrived, and Willie was now the man of the house – with responsibility for his mother and two wee sisters. He was only in his early teens but already he was a powerfully built lad, showing the signs of the big powerful man he was to grow into. As he tended the small flock of sheep the family had on the slopes of the hill called The Aud, he often found himself in tears remembering his father's last words to him.

'Mind now, Willie, look after your mum and the girls till I come back. It will be a grand day then with a new king and better times for all of us.'

Much of the time he was downcast and had no one he could speak to. When Ogilvy's regiment came back to same spot in the glen to disband in 1746, he watched from a distance, angry that his father seemed to have died in vain. He had been caught up in the excitement of the army being raised for the young Prince, but now he was just angry and confused. However, he knew that his father had been happy to go out to join the Prince's army and his real hatred was reserved for the Redcoats – the government soldiers who had come into the glen a week or so after the Regiment had disbanded. They had looted and pillaged most of the glen. Luckily, from Brocklas on the other side of the river from the road up the glen, the Mearns family had seen what was happening and had managed to drive their sheep and two cows up out of sight of the marauding troops before they arrived. Still, they had lost precious goods when the soldiers stormed through their home.

Willie and his sisters could only watch from the hills above as the soldiers ransacked the house. When a soldier knocked his mother to the ground he began to run down the hill, shouting to his sisters to mind the beasts but by the time he got there his mother was sitting alone at the front door, telling him 'Never mind, Willie I am all right'. All that day, smoke rose from houses up and down the glen as the troops set fire to haystacks, barns and houses.

The next day, Willie watched the troops march back out of the glen, some pushing carts laden with what they had looted, followed by horse-drawn carts piled high with booty, much of which was of little use to them and soon to be discarded. Willie's heart raced and his head pounded with the anger he felt, but what could a 12-year-old laddie do against 100 professional soldiers? Soldiers, he spat, they were nothing but bandits and thieves.

Within a few days though, Willie found there was something he could do. He was out on the Hill of Craigthran, near the headwaters of the Burn of Cuillt, when he saw something moving in a gorse bush at the side of the burn. At first he thought it was just a stoat or a weasel, but as he looked closer he saw that what had moved was an arm. Somebody was hiding in the gorse bushes. It could only be a rebel.

Now Willie was bright enough to approach the man carefully. If it was a rebel, and it had to be, the man would be armed and quite likely ready to shoot anyone he saw as a threat. Cautiously he approached the bush and quietly said, 'Hello?'

'Who is there?' came the reply and Willie saw a movement, realising by the movement in the bushes that the man had pointed a pistol in his direction. 'I am a friend,' Willie said quickly, 'my name is Willie and my father died for the Prince at Prestonpans.'

At that point the man groaned and Willie saw the pistol drop, He came forward and parted the bushes. There, lying on the ground was an unshaven, well-dressed man in a jacket, waistcoat and trews, and on the left side of his jacket an ominous dark, wet patch. Willie knew right off that the man was badly wounded.

'Here,' he said knelling by the man and pulling out his leather water bottle from the knapsack he carried with him, 'take a drink.'

The man reached for the bottle with his right arm and took it, raised it to his lips and gulped furiously. He then gave a cough and fell back, dropping the bottle. As he lay there he looked directly at Willie for the first time and gave a slight smile. 'Well, Willie, will ye help me?' he asked.

'I will do whatever I can,' said the lad. 'I have some bread and cheese here in my bag. Can you eat?'

The man nodded, and Willie gave him some bread and cheese which he gobbled down furiously. It was clear he had not eaten in some time. Once he had eaten he fell back again as if tired out with the effort, and his eyelids fluttered as if he would fall asleep. That was not a good idea, Willie thought and he said to the semi-comatose stranger, 'Look can you move? My home is less than two miles off and I can give you a hand. My mother will be able to take a look at your wound but if you stay here…'

The man looked him in the eye, 'Are there any Redcoats about?'

'There's a corporal and four men, but they are at the head of the glen and they never come down this far,' the young lad replied. 'If we wait till the gloaming and are careful, we can keep out of sight of the road for most of the way. Can you manage it?'

'It seems I have no real choice,' replied the man with a grim smile.

He was obviously in great pain and once the day had begun to fade it was a hard job for Willie to help him down the hillside. Most of the time he was virtually carrying the man. By the time they were close to Brocklas, the man's face was deathly white and his breath was coming in great laboured gasps. Willie was also aware that the damp patch on his left side was spreading. As they neared the house, one of Willie's sisters saw them coming and ran indoors to fetch her mother. She came running up the hill to give Willie a hand to carry the stranger the last couple of hundred yards to the house. By now, the last of the gloaming was on them and it would soon be dark. At the house, they carried him in to a simple box bed in the main room. As they laid him down he gave a groan and passed out.

Mrs Mearns looked at her son with a look he had never seen

before, but she only said, 'Fetch me hot water and get an old sheet from the kist, Willie. Girls, light a candle.'

Carefully in the soft light of the candles she cut the man's jacket away and undid his blood-soaked waistcoat. Under it his fine linen shirt was totally soaked with blood, much of it congealed but there was still some seeping through. She cut away the shirt to expose a hole in the man's side the size of a musket ball. Lifting him as gently as she could, she pulled the shirt from his back. There was a bigger hole which was oozing blood from round a half-formed scab. 'He's lucky,' she said, 'the ball went straight through. We can probably save him.'

So she cleaned and bandaged the wound and when she was done she draped a blanket over the man who had by now fallen into a deep, troubled sleep.

'Now girls,' she said, 'nobody is to hear we have this visitor, it is to be our secret and tomorrow and the days after I want you to keep an eye out for anyone coming to the house. If anyone does come you are to run and tell me. Do you understand?'

The two young lasses, Kirsty was nine and Isabel eight, nodded. They had seen enough trouble in their short lives to know that keeping this man's presence secret was important.

'All right then, have your supper and off to bed with the pair of you,' she said as she took off the clothes of the man in the bed. She proceeded to wash them in the big tub that sat at the front door before hanging them inside the house, all the time deep in thought and saying nothing to her son. He spent much of the time looking at the stranger in the bed and thinking of his father. Later though, the pair of them talked deep into the night. Before going to sleep Willie hid the man's clothing and his pistol in a hollow tree on the hillside above the house.

For the next few days, the girls kept an eye out as the man was fed with soup. By the second day, he was sitting up and managed to eat some lamb stew. It turned out he was from Edinburgh, a bookseller by trade, but his family were Episcopalians and he had headed west as soon as he had heard the Prince was raising his standard. After the disaster of Culloden, he had been heading south through Glen Esk towards Dundee where he had some friends, when he had been seen by a patrol and shot. He had tumbled down the bed of a stream and had managed to crawl nearly ten miles to where Willie found him.

For nearly a fortnight, the Mearns family took care of their visitor, and when at last he was ready to leave, he took a *sgian dubh* from inside his jacket and cut the 12 silver buttons off his waistcoat.

'These are for you,' he said giving six to Mrs Mearns and the other six to Willie, 'it is little enough for what you have done for me but you can sell these and live a little better in these hard times.'

Despite their protests that they were only giving him the necessary hospitality of tradition, he insisted they take the silver buttons. Taking Mrs Mearns by the hand, he smiled and said, 'If I had been found, you and Willie would have been jailed at the very least and well you know it. I am forever in your debt.'

And 100 years later, when Granny Mearns told the story to her grandchildren, she would pull out the last three of the silver buttons to show how true the story was.

The Canter of Coltbridge

When Charlie look't the letter upon
He drew his sword its scabbard from
Sayin, 'Follow me my merry men
We'll meet Johnnie Cope in the mornin.

When Johnnie Cope he heard o this
He thocht it widnae be amiss
Tae hae a horse in readiness
Tae gang awa in the mornin.'

TRADITIONAL SONG, LIKE STORY, is not overly concerned with historical accuracy. These verses from the well-known song 'Johnnie Cope,' reflect the generally accepted idea that the Battle of Prestonpans was a humiliating defeat for the British government. In reality the battle was brief and the British troops were routed as a result of the charge of the Highland troops. Just a day or so earlier however, some of the British troops had indeed run away at the very first sight of danger.

When Prince Charlie and his army approached Edinburgh on 16 September, there were a considerable number of Government troops in the area. Among them were two regiments of Dragoons, Gardiner's and Hamilton's. They were lined up at Coltbridge, nowadays Roseburn next to Murrayfield, but back then, open ground a mile or so from the city itself. By the thinking of the time, these dragoons armed with swords and state-of-the-art firearms should have had no problems facing a bunch of irregular troops armed mainly with swords and targes, with no formal military discipline at all. It was rumoured in the ranks of the British Army at the time that Highlanders were terrified of horses and could not stand before a cavalry charge. It was nothing but a rumour. Gardiner's Dragoons had already retreated from the Fords of Frew, east of Stirling when the Jacobite Army approached and they had come under fire.

As the Jacobite Army came towards Edinburgh, a scouting party of dragoons near Corstorphine saw the advance guard. When the Highlanders opened fire, the dragoons wheeled and galloped back to their comrades to let them know the enemy was coming. This caused panic in the ranks and Brigadier Fowkes, who had taken overall command, gave the order to wheel and head east. This was seen by the many spectators on the nearby hills who had come out from Edinburgh in anticipation of the expected battle, and by the garrison of the Castle. Locals talked for a long time after of the truly impressive military precision with which the body of horsemen executed this movement. Not a man was out of place and all the horses were perfectly in step as they rode together, away from the advancing enemy. It is said they made a beautiful sight as they headed back to Edinburgh.

Now, Edinburgh was a city divided in its loyalty. As many as half the population were supporters of the Jacobite cause. The Provost and most of the Town Council however were staunchly in the Hanoverian camp and were relying on the dragoons to protect their city, especially as it was already known that the Jacobites had only a handful of cavalry. The Castle was safe in the hands of a Government garrison.

As the dragoons headed back towards the castle, every so often they were commanded to increase speed. So it was that by the time they passed along the north edge of Edinburgh they were going at a fair old canter. As they passed through Barefoot's Parks on the then northern edge of the city, they were going at almost a gallop which caused some consternation among the locals as the heavy horses funneled through the narrow lanes. This sight was greeted with cheers and laughter by those of the Jacobite persuasion but brought fear into the hearts of the Hanoverians – were they being deserted by their protectors without a fight?

On the dragoons went towards the port of Leith without slackening their pace at all. On reaching the port they were at last brought to a halt by their commander. However no sooner had they drawn up in line on the links when a local lad came running and shouted,

'The Highlanders, the Highlanders are coming.' The capacity of these bold dragoons to respond to command was obvious at once as, to a man, they spurred their horses, and rode off at a furious pace – heading east. The wee lad, from a Jacobite family, fell about laughing as the brave dragoons rode off.

On they rode, passing through Leith, then on they went to Musselburgh, where they set up for the evening in a field near Colonel Gardiner's house, at Preston, the colonel taking up his quarters in his own dwelling. That night, some time between ten and eleven, one of the dragoons fell into one of the many disused coal pits in the area, while out looking for food for his horse. At once he shouted for help. His companions heard the shouting, but were unable to make out the words. They immediately assumed the worst: It must be the Highlanders approaching. With remarkable speed they gathered themselves together, mounted up and headed off towards Dunbar. Colonel Gardiner awoke in the morning to find that his troops had fled without him and went off after them. The Jacobites were delighted to tell that he had no problem trailing the dragoons as the road was strewn with pistols, swords and fire-locks, which had all been thrown aside as the panicked soldiers fled east! Good and steady soldier that he was, and realizing there was no sign of the Highlanders approaching, he arranged to have these picked up by locals, put in carts and sent on to Dunbar where he arrived in time to meet General Cope who had just landed. The arms were distributed to the sheepish dragoons, but they did them little good for many of them were killed in the rout at Prestonpans the following day, a battle in which Gardiner fought bravely till he died.

The Coltbridge Canter provides some of the scenes in the recently completed Prestonpans Tapestry commemorating this famous Jacobite victory.

A True Heroine

DAVID OGILVY WAS THE SON of the Earl of Airlie and he raised a regiment to fight for the Jacobite cause in 1745. His father, showing that canny awareness that has served Scottish lairds so well, stayed at home, and later claimed to be a loyal Hanoverian, thus saving his lands. David fled the country after the disaster of Culloden, and after journeying in secret to Scandinavia, finally found safety in France. His wife, Lady Ogilvy, born Margaret Johnstone, of Auchterhouse, was not only an outstanding beauty but, as her actions showed, she was also a woman of remarkable strength of character. She was one of the belles of the ball at Prince Charles Edward Stewart's short-lived court in Edinburgh, and she accompanied the Jacobite army on its ill-fated foray into England. In fact, it is said she was such a brave woman that she thought little of standing on the battlefield holding the reins of a spare horse for her husband in case he needed it.

During the retreat from Derby she was sent ahead of the main body of troops in a coach with a substantial mounted escort. Somehow, a rumour started that the coach in fact contained the prince and a great deal of gold! This was probably the cause of the attack on the coach that took place at Lancaster, in which three people were killed. The assailants, not Government troops, were driven off, and Margaret was unharmed.

Now, at this time both the Government and the Jacobites had extensive intelligence networks throughout England and Scotland, and on their way north Lady Ogilvy's party heard that there was another ambush planned near Perth. It seemed that someone with the party was sending information ahead of them so she returned to the main body of the army.

On their way north, in January 1746, the Jacobite army laid siege to Stirling Castle. An army led by General Henry Hawley was approaching from the south. Most of the Jacobite army set off to meet the approaching forces and had their last victory, such as it was, at the Battle of Falkirk on the 17th. After this, they headed north, picking up the troops besieging the castle as they went. Nobody, however, told Lady Ogilvy what was happening, and she woke up a couple of days later in the inn where she was staying to find the town of Stirling filling up with Hawley's troop, who had re-formed, and, having been reinforced with more troops, were following the Jacobite army. Her coach was outside the inn, and, still in bed, she could hear the sound of a troop of Government soldiers surrounding it. As quick thinking as she was brave, she moved quickly and headed out of the back of the inn and along the road out of town. She had dressed herself in spare clothes belonging to her maid, leaving her own rich dresses hidden under a bed. Luckily, she also had some money, and soon, she and her maid had managed to get horses and were riding off after the Jacobite army. We can imagine the words she had with her husband for abandoning her to the not so tender mercies of the Government troops.

On 16 April 1746 she was on Drumossie Moor, once more holding a spare horse for her husband, when the unfortunate tactics of the prince and his advisers led the Jacobites into the hellish slaughter of Culloden. Once the battle was lost she headed off to a friend's house not far away but was soon identified and captured. Probably because of her status, she was not subjected to the brutality that so many Scots women underwent at the hands of the Government forces and was sent to the prison in Inverness. Prisons in those days were truly grim places. While there, she heard the uplifting news that her husband had managed to escape to the Continent. After two months here she was escorted to Edinburgh, where at least she would be more comfortable in the castle than in Inverness Gaol. As a notable aristocrat, and one who had played such an important role at the prince's court, the Government intended making an example of her. They didn't, however, allow for her courage and intelligence.

While she was locked up in Edinburgh Castle, Lady Ogilvy was visited regularly, by her sister Barbara, who lived in Edinburgh. Barbara had arranged for a local woman to handle Lady Ogilvy's laundry. The laundress was soon a regular sight coming and going at the castle. She had an assistant, a young lass who carried the laundry up to the castle gate for her, but was not allowed in. The laundress herself was an older woman who had been born with a twisted back and walked with a very pronounced limp. On one occasion, after delivering the clean laundry, she was about to leave the cell when Lady Ogilvy spoke. 'You have a strange way of walking, would you mind if I tried to walk the same way?' she asked with a smile.

'Well, if it pleases your Ladyship, I can see no harm in it,' replied the bemused laundress, thinking to herself, 'It's right enough what they say about the nobility, they are gey queer.'

So, over the next few visits Lady Ogilvy was coached in how to limp like the laundress. She then broached her plan to the laundress and asked her to smuggle in a spare set of her own clothes amongst the laundry over the course of the next week.

A day or so later, in the evening, the warden came to Lady Ogilvy's cell with a servant carrying her evening meal. He met Barbara at the door of her sister's quarters. 'I am sorry,' she said. 'My sister is unwell. She does not want any food. If you don't mind, I will stay here tonight and keep her company. She really isn't well at all.'

The warden agreed to let her stay. Barbara went back in the cell, and he heard her whispering to her sister. Barbara then came back to the cell door and quietly wished the warden a goodnight. In the morning, when her breakfast was brought, Barbara said she had had a bad night but had fallen asleep and seemed to be more peaceful now. It wasn't until the following day, a Monday, that the truth was discovered. The guards on the gate of the castle had not noticed that two limping maids had gone down the hill on the Saturday evening – and why should they? It had been carefully arranged that Lady Ogilvy, dressed in the laundress's clothes and feigning her limp and hunched way of walking, would go out of the castle first, and the old woman would follow after the guard on the gate was changed. Lady Ogilvy had simply changed into the laundress's clothes, pulled the shawl over her head, lifted the laundry basket and hobbled her way down to the gate to join the young lass outside the castle. None of the guards paid any attention to the crippled figure passing by them, and, once the pair of them were clear of the castle, they turned into one of the many wynds leading off the High Street and disappeared from view. The young lass was a bit taken aback at her mistress's silence as she was normally keen to chat about her visits to Lady Ogilvy. You can imagine her surprise when, once they were a fair distance from the castle, the old crooked lady whipped off her shawl and stood up, revealing herself to be a graceful and beautiful young woman. She took the young lass's hand and pressed some silver coins into the astounded young girl's hand. Then she spoke.

'Now, you will not tell anyone of this, will you? Your mistress said you were a fine lass and that I can count on you.'

The lassie could only nod agreement, being totally lost for words. Lady Ogilvy smiled at her companion, winked broadly, and ran off! She then made her way down the Royal Mile to a friend's house in Abbey Hill, where a set of men's clothing and a horse were waiting for her, as was her personal maid. Lingering only long enough to say farewell to Lady Ogilvy's faithful friends, the pair of them set off south. They did not take the road to London, where the chances of being recognised and arrested were considerable, as Lady Ogilvy saw no point in exchanging the confines of Edinburgh Castle for Tower Hill. Instead, they made their way, by back roads whenever possible, down the east coast to Hull, where there was a ship waiting to take them on to Rotterdam. At last, Lady Ogilvy and her maid boarded the ship that was to take them to safety on the Continent. But even this was not the end of her adventures. Yet again, a rumour sprang up that the gentleman who had boarded the ship was in fact Prince Charlie himself! A search party of soldiers was sent for and came onboard the ship. Luckily, Lady Ogilvy and her maid were aware of what was about to happen. So, when the soldiers appeared on the deck of the ship, they were met by her maid. She told them that this was no prince but merely her mistress, who had fallen into debt and was heading abroad to avoid bringing her family into disgrace. When she opened the door of the cabin to show the beautiful Lady

Ogilvy sitting at a table in a fancy gown, with her shoulders and upper bosom bare, none of the soldiers had any doubt that this was no man! She escaped to the Low Countries and headed to France where she was soon re-united with David.

This, though, was still not the end of Margaret's adventures. In 1751, she found out that she was carrying a child. She and David realised that if the son they were hoping for was to have any hope of ever succeeding to his grandfather's estates, it was imperative that he was born in Scotland. So, heavily pregnant, she returned to Scotland in disguise. In her own family's house at Auchterhouse, not far from Dundee, she was delivered of her baby. To everyone's delight it was a boy, and a day later, his birth was registered by her father. She knew that she could not remain in Scotland. If she did it would only be a matter of time before she was arrested and jailed, or worse! So, a few weeks later, a tearful Lady Ogilvy said farewell to her newborn son and went back to France.

He was to be brought up by his grandparents and in time would succeed to the title and lands that were his due, but Lady Ogilvie realised that she would most likely never see her child again. And so it was, for she died at Boulogne in 1757 without setting eyes on her child or her native land again. As for the son she had risked liberty, and perhaps life, to have, her son born in her native land, he grew up severely mentally impaired and never did succeed his grandfather. Her last great adventure had been for nothing.

Ardshiel

CHARLES STEWART OF ARDSHIEL looked down on his house from the slopes of Beinn a Bheithir. Having left the horrors of Culloden Moor less than a week before, now he saw further problems. His house, a substantial two storey stone building with a tiled roof, looking out over the waters of Loch Linnhe was much different from the humble heather-thatched black houses of the clanspeople whose chieftain he was. Many of the loyal clansmen who had followed him from those houses lay dead on Culloden Moor or were awaiting their fate as prisoners of the rampant British Army. And he could clearly see that Ardshiel House was now in the hands of the red-coated soldiers.

The horror of the defeat at Culloden and its brutal aftermath lay heavily on Ardshiel's mind. He had led his clansmen through the campaign into England and back again all this way, for what? Decision after decision by Prince Charles had been wrong and the infighting between him and Lord George Murray had been heart-breaking. No wonder there had been such slaughter. Now though, with the Jacobite cause in tatters, certainly for the time being, he had best look to himself. As one of the leaders of the attempt to regain the throne for the Stewarts he knew well that, if he was captured, he would be executed. There was no doubt about that. So, what to do? The most obvious thing to do was to join the other chiefs and leaders who were trying to get to France. With the help of the prince, he could perhaps find a role either at the court of King James or perhaps in the French Army. There he could bide his time and await the next stage of the campaign. Although he was angry at what he saw was bad leadership, he had little doubt that the Prince would be back and if this time he actually managed to have proper French support, matters would be different. And in his heart there was cold rage, for he wanted to go into battle once more against the British Army. He had heard of the slaughter of the wounded and the widespread rape and pillage that was going on throughout the Highlands by the specific orders of the King's son, the Duke of Cumberland.

He was in despair that he could do nothing to help his own people who were even now suffering at the hands of the soldiers. He knew he was helpless and should set his mind on getting to France as soon as possible. But he couldn't go without seeing his pregnant wife and children, for the chances were that he wouldn't see them for a long, long time, if ever again. It was all bad.

Beside Charles were MacColl of Glen Stocadal and Stewart of Invernahyle who had come with him from the battlefield. Their thoughts too, were on the mistakes of the past months, the problems of their immediate future and their total inability to do anything to help their suffering people. They said little. Sticking to the high ground it had taken them the better part of a week to make it to Appin. As they came over Beinn a Bheithir, they had clearly seen the men in red coats around the house. The Duke of Cumberland had wasted no time. He had despatched soldiers to the homes of all known leaders of the rising in the hope of capturing at least some of them. And the soldiers at Ardshiel were under the command of Captain Caroline Scott, a man whose sadistic brutality was already marking him out as one of the most scabrous creatures ever to have been born in Scotland. Still, Charles had no intention of leaving Scotland without saying farewell to his family, no matter the danger.

'Stop this,' he said to himself, 'this is no time to be brooding.' Turning to motion his companions to follow, he headed to a nearby house high up on Beinn a Bheithir where the woman of the house was more than glad to see her chief and feed him and his friends, especially when she heard that her husband too had managed to escape from the slaughter on Drummossie Moor. After a meal of the simple food that she had, Stocadal and Invernahyle left to try and see their own families. The woman then said she was ready to take a message from Ardshiel to his lady. Later that April day, as the evening came on, Ardshiel was hiding in his own barn when his wife Isobel and one of his daughters came in. As he took his wife in his arms he could feel the tears streaming down her face.

'Daddy, daddy,' whispered his daughter, standing at the door of the barn, 'soldiers are coming!'

Quickly he dived into a pile of hay and his daughter sat on top if it playing with the little doll she had brought with her. In strode Captain Scott, a pistol in his hand. Seeing the child playing on the hay and her mother standing quite still looking distracted, and with tears clearly on her cheeks, the soldier had a quick look round, and told them to get out of the barn. 'Tell your mother I'll meet you in the garden,' whispered Stewart to his wee lass from his hiding place.

The sense of danger seemed to give Ardshiel heightened senses. He could hear the soldiers all around. Once his wife and child had followed the soldier out of the barn he crawled out of the hay and looked through a chink in the barn wall. Biding his time he waited till the coast was clear and made a run for the garden. He was crouching down beside the kale patch when his wife came towards him, but he had to throw himself into the kale as he saw the lurking figure of Scott behind her. Scott clearly realised that Charles would to try to get in contact with his wife. She turned away from the garden and headed back to the house, Scott still dogging her footsteps. All around the house there were Redcoats, but Charles had lived there all his life and managed to get away without being seen. Once clear of the house, he headed back up to Beinn a Bheithir, going to a cave hidden behind the waterfall at Lag-na-ha, above the village of Kentallen. Here he remained for many months, while the area was combed by soldiers, but they never found him. Even today, if you don't know exactly where you are going, the cave is hard to find. Although damp at the front, it is dry at the back away from the waterfall, and it stretches back almost 20 feet. Someone standing five yards away would not see it. A rough hideout, but it served Ardshiel well.

Over the next few days he ventured out very occasionally. Food was brought to him by a young lass who was up on the hill every day looking after the sheep, which as yet had not been 'requisitioned' by Scott and his men. A few days later Scott went off suddenly with his troops and Charles took the chance to hurry down to Ardshiel House for a tearful reunion with his wife and family. He wasn't in the house more than an hour, however, before word came that the soldiers were returning. Off he sped, back to his cave. Several times more he crept down to the house under the cover of darkness to capture a few sweet moments with his wife, who was well into her pregnancy by now, but it was never more than a fleeting few moments.

Food was brought to him on other occasions by some of his clansmen on the hillside cutting osiers to make baskets but always he had to be extremely careful. If Scott or his soldiers ever found out about the cave he was he would be trapped with no means of escape. Meanwhile, Scott was becoming more and more angry with the situation. He had no doubt that Ardshiel was nearby but despite the brutality of his men, he could not get anyone locally to tell him a single thing about their chief's whereabouts. In a vain attempt to encourage co-operation, he began to burn the houses of those who wouldn't tell him what he wanted to hear. And then he began to take the livestock and send it off to Fort William to be sold. Still no one would tell him where Ardshiel was hiding and he refused to believe he had already left the country. At last, in August, he proceeded to strip Ardshiel House. First he took all the furniture, linen, books and other possessions of the family, including the children's schoolbooks. Then he had his men remove the windows, doors, wall fittings, chandeliers, everything, including the slates from the roof. He even had his men straighten out the nails that held the woodwork together, sending them off to Fort William to be sold. Then with the cruelty for which he has been long remembered, he asked Lady Stewart for the house keys. Isobel had no choice but to obey. Then Scott offered his hand in a parody of gentlemanly behaviour then led her out of the door of Ardshiel surrounded by her terrified children and said, 'Now go, you damn rebel bitch, you have no business here any more.'

It was then Isobel's true mettle shone through. She looked the soldier straight in the eye, and said, 'I am going nowhere. This is my home and the home of my children. What kind of man are you that you would turn us out defenceless and with no food?'

Shamed by the woman's courage Scott cursed and rode away leaving a sack of meal. He took some of his troops but left a small detachment to keep watch in case Ardshiel should return. There were also other troops in the immediate area and the search for Ardshiel did not diminish even as Scott rode off to harass and harry others of his countrymen.

One morning, only a few weeks after this, one of the young lads who had been taking food to Ardshiel saw a troop of soldiers heading towards Beinn a Bheithir. He suspected that somehow they had heard of Ardshiel's cave. The boy, Lachlan, was only ten years old but he was well aware of all that was going on around him. He followed the soldiers as they headed towards the south-western slopes of the mountain towards where Lag-na-ha was. When the soldiers stopped to eat at midday he ran uphill through the heather, then came down the hill towards the detachment. He had noticed a drummer boy sitting at the edge of the troops. Lachlan had only a few words of English, but boys are boys everywhere, and when he came up to the wee drummer boy who was hardly older than he was, they nodded at each other. He sat down, and, using signs and the few English words he knew, he let the boy soldier know that he 'had always wanted to be a soldier himself and that he thought his drum was beautiful. The young drummer boy felt flattered and handed over his drum for Lachlan to look at. He turned it over in his hands, as if it were a truly magic thing then he made signs to the other boy asking if he could try and tap it. Unwittingly the drummer boy handed over his drumsticks and at once Lachlan thundered away on the drum. At once a sergeant ran over and slapped the sticks from his hands and gave him a terrible thwack around the ear. The wee drummer boy shot to his feet and stood to attention as he was shouted at for being such a fool. The gist of the sergeant's words, amongst the curses, was the fact that you couldn't trust any of these Highland savages.

The soldiers then headed off, leaving Lachlan feeling sick and dizzy in the heather. But his ploy had worked. Ardshiel had heard and realising how close the sound was, had left the cave at Lag-na-ha and had headed up to the summit of Beinn a Bheithir. There he lay and watched as the troops came round the side of the hill and passed within yards of his hideout. This time, they hadn't found the cave, but as they searched across the mountainside, he realised that the time had come for him to leave. So in the early days of September, Ardsheil made a last secret visit to his home and bid a tearful farewell to his wife and children. He felt terrible for leaving them, particularly as Isobel only had two months to go till she gave birth, but they both knew he had to go. So with the help of some faithful clansmen he made his way north and a week or so later, after having to dodge several more patrols, Charles Stewart of Ardshiel boarded a ship at Peterhead and sailed for France, never to see his home again.

Captain Caroline Scott however, had not yet finished with the Stewart family. In December, just as she was due to give birth, Isobel Stewart received another visit from Scott. Winter had come and the ground was covered with snow as the bold captain rode up to Ardshiel House where Isobel and the children were just managing to survive in one of the gutted rooms. This time, he turned them all out of the house and set fire to it. As the house blazed to the dark sky Isobel was forced to head off to a nearby barn where, that night, she gave birth. The next night Scott and some of his fellow officers came to where she was lying and cursed her husband for a fool for deserting her in her hour of need.

Later she managed to make her way with her children to France to be with her husband, leaving the estate management in the loyal hands of James of the Glen until he was removed and the estate taken over by the Hanoverians. Even after this, the tenants remained loyal to their hereditary chief and continued to send rents to Ardshiel and Isobel in France, as well as paying rent to the crown. Many years later, Charles' son, Duncan, managed to regain the family lands, but by then, his father had died in France, never again looking out from the slopes of Beinn a Bheithir over Loch Linnhe and the ancestral lands of his fathers.

Away from Tilbury

IN THE AFTERMATH of Culloden, many Jacobite prisoners were sent to London. Almost 300 of them were put aboard old transport ships anchored in the Thames off the Fort at Tilbury. These ancient, rotting ships were filthy and in the closed in spaces between decks disease was rife. By September 1746, nearly one in six of these prisoners had died. One in 20 of them, chosen by lot, were put on trial and virtually all of these were executed, some by the barbaric method of being hung, drawn and quartered. The survivors were eventually sent off to the West Indies to work as slaves in the sugar plantations and though some survived this, many died under the hot tropical sun, or of disease. Being sent to Tilbury was the next best thing to a death sentence. There was however, one man who did manage to escape, Stewart Carmichael of Bonnyhaugh. He had been arrested in September 1746 along with Sir James Stewart of Burray, on suspicion of being a Jacobite. In those troubled times, merely being suspected of sympathising with the Stewart cause was enough to have you thrown into prison. Some people were imprisoned for simply drinking to Prince Charlie's health and that alone could, and did, lead to transportation or death. The brutality of the crackdown by the British Government was horrific. Although Carmichael and Stewart were arrested in Scotland, the pair of them were sent down to London and we can only imagine their horror at being sent on to a rotting, stinking hulk in the Thames. The well-known motto from Dante's Inferno 'Abandon Hope All Ye Who Enter Here' seems to be a fitting description of what they must have felt.

The brutality shown towards the prisoners extended to their keep and feeding. The ships were freezing cold in winter, boiling hot in summer and the dank, foetid air in the holds and between the lower decks where they were locked up, meant even the strongest were susceptible to a horrendous range of diseases. And as these were rebels against the King and government, the food they were given was the very worst. The regular fare was offal, often from diseased cattle and pigs, sent out from the market at Gravesend. Money was of course being made by the speculators supplying such grim fare on government contracts, but there was no one who would listen to the prisoners' complaints if the so-called foodstuffs being sent out to the ship was actually inedible. At this time, the quality of food even in the Royal Navy was quite atrocious, so what victuals the Jacobite prisoners actually had to eat can only be imagined. However, as it was mainly offal that was being sent to the hulks, Carmichael had a brain wave.

Given the pitiful condition of the prisoners, and the fact that the hulks were out in the middle of the River Thames, the guards on the ships were not particularly observant; the idea that anyone would try to escape seemed pretty far-fetched. But Carmichael had no intention of giving up the ghost. He was a young man, barely in his 20s and knew if he wanted to escape he had to do it while he was still healthy. Back in those days, before tin cans had been invented and glass was very expensive, one of the standard ways of transporting liquid was inside animal bladders. The illicit whisky makers of Scotland had long used bladders to shift their produce, a secondary advantage of bladders being that they could easily be hidden, not only in milk churns and amongst hay and vegetables, but also under peoples' clothing. It may be that it was this use of bladders that gave Carmichael his idea. He noticed soon after arrival that the deliveries of offal often had the bladders of the animals still attached, and these were generally discarded before the entrails were boiled up in great vats to form a sort of gruel to feed the prisoners.

So, keeping a weather eye open at all times, Carmichael managed to get hold of a bladder. We can only hope he managed to clean it up before hiding it, though any smell it did give off, would probably not have been noticed by any of the jailers who very sporadically came into the cramped and filthy quarters of the prisoners. Having checked that his bladder was airtight, Carmichael bided his time till he could get another one, then another and another. When he had four bladders he could at last put his plan into action.

During many nights while the rest of his fellow prisoners were asleep he had picked away with a nail at the door frame of the hold he was kept in. The ancient ship had long been moored in the Thames and the passing of the years and the damp had made much of the wood soft. So he had carefully weakened the door frame till he could pull it, and the door itself, free of the surrounding wall. Waiting till a night when he could hear a steady downpour of rain, he made his move. With the rain falling he knew there would be little or no visibility, so if he got over the ship's side there was little likelihood of him being seen. And the noise of the rain would help dampen any sounds he himself made. So he gathered up his bladders and went to the door. Slowly, making as little noise as he could, he tugged at the door frame till it came free. Pulling it back just enough to make space for himself he pushed the bladders through and then wriggled through the space he had created. Once through, he did his best to pull the frame back as close as he could to its original position. Then, picking up his bladders, he quietly made his way up to the ship's deck. With the steady rain coming down, he saw there was no one on deck other than a figure hunched close to a lamp about 40 feet away, near the ship's bow. By the look of him the man was sound asleep anyway. Carmichael took a deep breath and began to inflate his first bladder. Within a few minutes he had all four inflated and tied them together with strips of cloth he had torn from his shirt. Then, hooking the bladders under his armpits he climbed the gunwale and clambered down the outside of the ship. The shock of the cold water made him gasp as he slid in but he was exhilarated, his heart was pounding and his breath was coming in short bursts. He pushed himself off from the ship's side. Hoping that his memory was not playing tricks he pointed his head towards where he thought the north shore of the river was and began to kick. The tide caught him but he was being kept buoyant by the bladders and his powerful kicks kept him going constantly, if slowly towards the river bank. Within half an hour he came to land and pulled himself ashore.

Drenched to the skin, he looked terrible but there were few people about and as he walked back towards London, hugging himself to try and stop shivering he didn't look much worse than the few poor individuals who he passed in the steady rain. He had friends in London he could call on, friends who he was certain would help him.

Within a few hours he was in one such friend's house, a fellow Jacobite who was only too pleased to help, once he had got over the shock of finding the utterly bedraggled and shivering Carmichael on his doorstep. He stayed hidden for a few weeks, before sending word home. In time a message came back with enough money to help him leave the country. He didn't know if he was a wanted man, or if he had even been missed but he knew he still had to be careful. Every day, there were executions of Jacobite prisoners down at Tilbury. And so it was that he ended up fleeing London on a ship to, of all places, Jamaica. However he was not going in chains as an 'indentured servant', which was what so many of the prisoners were called as they entered years of slavery, but as a free man. He was the only Jacobite prisoner who ever made it out of the Tilbury hulks alive, and there were many warm Jamaican nights when he thought sadly of the poor unfortunate souls he had left behind.

James Davidson

IN THE 18TH CENTURY, many Scots enlisted in the armies and navies of Austria, France, Italy, Prussia, Russia, Spain and Sweden. This was happening even before the Jacobite cause gained strength. However, there was also a tradition of serving in the British Army. While this may have often been due more to economic circumstances than any particular loyalty to the British state, it was a well established practice, and in the aftermath of Prince Charlie raising his standard at Glenfinnan, many such men deserted to join the Jacobite army in Scotland. One of these was James Davidson, a man hailing originally from Brechin, and though not a Highlander himself he was among the 'braw lads in the heather' who refused to surrender after the horrors of Culloden. In truth, many of them thought that Culloden was just one lost battle, and hadn't they won the three before that? Surely the Prince would be coming back, and if he brought French soldiers with him they could still win. It was many years before such ideas finally faded away and the number of British army troops stationed in Scotland for the next decade showed that the government too thought the Prince's return possible, if not probable. And they were all too aware of the level of support for the Jacobite cause that continued to exist in many parts of Scottish society. Meantime these men had to survive and the old raiding practices would serve them well. It has to be said, however, that some of these lads were inclined to do a bit more than simply sustain themselves. While the government classed them all as simple thieves, most of them were simply trying to keep the cause going, although some were undoubtedly simple bandits. And James Davidson it seems had inclinations that way.

Now, it would be totally false to say that all of Scotland supported the Jacobite cause. Although support was strong, particularly in the North East and much of the Highlands, there were those who were loyal to the Hanoverian crown and this was often due as much to religious persuasion as anything else. It was a fact that many Presbyterian ministers saw the Hanoverians as protectors of their own religion and a bulwark against any possible return of Catholicism. Many of them preached from their pulpits against the Catholic Stewart dynasty and the Jacobite cause. This in turn meant that many of the Jacobites, both Episcopalian and Catholic, saw them as their sworn enemies. They were thus potential targets and, as few of them were in the habit of keeping weapons about their manses, they were easy pickings for the less scrupulous of the lads in the heather. And James was surely one of those. While other Jacobites at the time stuck relatively closely to the old clan tradition of lifting cattle, though now selling on any they didn't actually eat themselves, James and his cronies had a different approach. With a handful of companions he made it his business to rob ministers.

In 1747, they raided the home of the Reverend Robert Melville at Durris. Like many other Presbyterian ministers, Melville had often spoken against the Jacobites from the pulpit and, according to James, this made him fair game. They broke into his manse in the night and stole everything of value they could find, threatening the minister with violence if he got on their way. That was bad enough but Mrs Melville, who was close to giving birth at the time, had died within a day of the raid. Most people in the area believed it was down to the shock of being robbed in the middle of the night. This was not the kind of behaviour to endear Davidson and his gang to the local population, no matter what their political sympathies may have been. Over the next year, they roamed the north-east and stole large sums of money, twenty-five pounds from the Kinkell minister and thirty-eight pounds from the schoolmaster at Durris. This was a particulary large sum and probably the man's life savings, but that matters little to a thief, though why should they target a schoolmaster? Was he a prominent Hanoverian supporter or did they just know he had money?

While it seems fair to think of others who stayed out after Culloden and survived by cattle raiding, as something like modern guerrilla fighters, Davidson and his gang's activities made it highly unlikely that they would find support from the population. Ministers, even if they were supporters of the Hanoverian cause, were generally considered decent and respectable people and by targeting them, James Davidson was giving justification to the Government's attempt to brand all the remaining Jacobites as thieves!

In 1748, Davidson and two others came to Cortachy, just south of the Angus glens of Clova and Prosen, just north of where the Earls of Airlie have long had their castle at Cortachy. Here, they met their match and although his two companions fought their way free when the locals rose against them, James Davidson was captured by two local men, David Moodie and James Kynoch.

First Davidson was sent to Perth prison, then from there to Edinburgh before it was decided he should be sent to Aberdeen, close to where he had committed most of his crimes. He was tried and the verdict was never in doubt, and nor was the sentence. He was to be hanged as a thief. However, there was one thing that certainly could be said of James Davidson. He was a man of strong character, or to put it in another way, he certainly had a brass neck! On the scaffold just before he was hung, he boldly stated, 'I am no thief, I am simply a man, loyal to the true king who did no more than harass his enemies.'

Gypsy Donald

AMONG THE JACOBITES who stayed out around Braemar was a famous Highland warrior called Gypsy Donald. Whether he was originally one of Scotland's travelling folk or not isn't clear, but everyone knew him as *Donald-Dubh-an-t-Ephiteach*, the Gaelic term for gypsy – literally translated as Dark Donald the Egyptian. He had a reputation as a fierce fighting man and he had been to the fore in many of the inter-clan skirmishes that regularly took place in the first half of the 17th century on Deeside. His loyalty was to the Farquharson clan and the clan chief, Farquharson of Invercauld knew he could always call on Donald Dubh in time of trouble. Now, in the months and years after Culloden, Deeside, like most of Scotland, was heavily garrisoned by the British Army. Most of these garrisons were by English troops. In the Highlands, this was supposedly to try and stop the activities of cattle thieves, but this was simply how the government described the 'Braw Lads' who stayed out in the heather refusing to give up the Jacobite cause. Most of them survived by using the traditional cattle raiding skills they had learned as young men though, despite the pillaging and persecution of the population they could always rely on some level of support from the locals, who were often of course their relatives. The destruction and pillage that had been visited on the Highlands after the Battle of Culloden on Drumossie Moor had effectively destroyed traditional clan life and the Duke of Cumberland had actively encouraged his soldiers to take all the livestock they could find. Of course, with government backing this cannot be construed as theft, and for many months in 1746 there was an almost permanent cattle market at Fort Augustus as the common soldiers brought in the cattle, sheep and horses that they had managed to acquire. This in turn meant that the lads in the heather were forced to raid outside the Highlands and the subsequent raiding in the Lowland areas gave some justification to the government's categorising of them all as thieves. In modern terms of course they were simply guerrilla fighters.

Now the biggest British Army garrison in the area was at Braemar Castle and at one point in the late 1740s there was a sergeant stationed there, who for some reason, took a personal dislike towards Donald. They had never met, but the sergeant was well aware of the respect that the local people had for Donald. As time went by, he became more and more frustrated that neither he nor any of his comrades could lay their hands on the Jacobite. So the sergeant took it into his head to try and get at Donald through his widowed mother, whose wee cottage sat near the foot of a hill called Morrone, less then two miles south east of Braemar. He would barge in to her house, demand to be fed and then he would insult her son, boasting of what he would do to him when he eventually caught up with him. Now this sergeant was well known for having been heavily involved in the killing of wounded Jacobites immediately after Culloden and was a man who showed no mercy to anyone he considered his enemy, or his king's. He was hated by all of the people of Deeside, and, though a bully, no one thought of him as a coward. Like Donald himself he was a tall, strong and athletic man and absolutely convinced that he was a match for any Highland savage.

One night after many such visits, Donald's mother had apparently had enough. Family has always been of great importance in Highland society and the unending insults directed at her son, and all other Highlanders, seemed to have worn her down. She looked up at the sergeant from her stool beside the peat fire.

'You keep telling me,' she said in halting English, 'that you are more than a match for my son and that all you wish is for a chance to meet him man for man. It is time that you had your chance.'

'What do you mean, woman?' the soldier demanded.

'I mean that I have arranged for you to meet my son if you have the courage to face him alone, with just your sword,' came the reply.

Now, bully and sadist though he was, the man had some sense of honour.

'Name the time and place and I will meet your great brave son, man for man,' he sneered, 'just be sure to have his shroud ready.'

'He will meet you this very evening up at Coire nam Muc,' she said, 'I know that he is waiting for you right now.' The sergeant let out a laugh and placing his musket by the door, left the cottage and headed up towards the corrie on the slope of Morrone.

As soon as he was out of the door there was a movement on top of the big box bed that sat against the wall of the room. It was Gypsy Donald himself, who had been lying there listening to every word.

'Do not worry mother,' he said, 'I will have the better of this evil braggart'

'I know that son,' his mother replied with a smile, and he went off after the soldier.

His familiarity with his home ground meant that by the time the sergeant got to Coire nam Muc, Donald was waiting for him.

'I see you came alone,' shouted the sergeant, 'well you will soon regret that.' And, pulling out his sword he flew at Donald. Donald had his own sword in his hand and soon they were hard at it. The sergeant quickly realised that the man he was fighting was every bit as powerful as himself, and that he certainly knew how to fight with a sword. He wasted no breath on insulting his foe, all his energy and concentration were focused on one thing – killing the man in front of him. At first, the sergeant's attack had made Donald fall back slightly but it was only a minute or two before he began to drive the Englishman back. The sergeant fought furiously but soon began to realise he had met his match. Then, with a deft twist Donald caught the handle of the sergeant's sword with his own point, and tore the weapon from his grasp, closing in fast to strike him on the head with the pommel of his sword. The soldier fell unconscious on the spot. He awoke to find himself lying in the heather with his hands tied behind him, and the tall, dark Highlander standing impassively over him with his arms folded.

'Well then sergeant, if you had me now where I have you, what would you do?'

No one had ever doubted the sergeant's courage and he spoke, truthfully if dangerously.

'I should kill you.' he said simply.

'Ach well then,' said Donald slowly. 'Maybe that's what I should do to you after how you treated my friends on Drummossie Moor, but, as you have been so honest I will spare your life. But you will remember me for as long as you live.'

He hauled the man to his feet, and holding his sword to the man's throat cut his bonds with his dirk. He told the man to get undressed and once he had done so, he retied his hands. Then, tying up the soldier's clothes in a bundle and hanging it round his neck, he reached down into the heather and lifted up a bunch of birch twigs, which he had obviously prepared beforehand. He then proceeded to march the man back down the slopes of Morrone thrashing him all the way. He didn't let up until they were only a few hundred yards from Braemar Castle itself, where he left him and returned to the hills.

When the sergeant staggered into the Castle there was uproar and a patrol was sent out immediately, but they could find no sign of Gypsy Donald. Over the next few weeks, the patrols were increased as the Commander of the Castle attempted to bring in the man who had so gravely insulted the whole British Army by his actions. It was notable that even after he had recovered from his thrashing, the sergeant was not to the fore on these expeditions. They never did manage to catch Gypsy Donald, and after general amnesty had been declared, he returned home and lived to a ripe old age and at last died in his own bed in what had been his mother's house.

An Old Man on the Run

BONNIE PRINCE CHARLIE is often represented as an ideal hero, young, handsome, charismatic and courageous. While it is clear he was all of these things, not all of those who came out in support of the '45 were as young, or as dashing as he was. One such Scot, who had been a staunch Jacobite since even before Charles' birth, was Alexander Forbes the 4th Lord Pitsligo. He had been out in the '15 with Mart after which he had spent many years in exile on the continent. In 1720, he had been allowed to return to his estate on the Buchan coast, but when the Prince raised his standard at Glenfinnan his old loyalty to those he regarded as the rightful kings of Britain reasserted itself and he joined the Jacobite army just after the Battle of Prestonpans. Although by then he was 67 years old and suffering from asthma, he rallied to the Jacobite cause, bringing a detachment of a hundred men from his estate with him. As he left Pitsligo had to be helped on to his horse, and was lectured by his wife of many decades, who tried to stop him going by reminding him that Mar's rebellion had ended in disaster.

'Ach well,' he replied, 'there never was a bridal yet but the second day was best,' and blew her a kiss as he rode off. He was known as a deep thinker and was much taken with the Christian mystic doctrine of Quietism, and though he had no great love for any of the Stewarts as such, he believed that they had been deposed unlawfully and his conscience would not let him stand by as the battle for the control of the British State raged.

Somehow, he managed to stay with the army throughout the campaign in England, even though he could play no real part in battle, and in the aftermath of the final battle he made his way from Culloden back along the coast towards Pitsligo. As one of Scotland's leading noblemen however, his participation in the rising had been well documented and the Government intended to make an example of him, particularly as he had already been pardoned for his earlier act of rebellion. There were Redcoats everywhere and to head straight back to Pitsligo Castle would have been madness.

So in the cold spring of 1746 he hid out in the mountains, often on his own, and living on little but oats and water. This had long been a staple of Highland diet but things were so bad they could not even get salt, and no Highlander has ever liked his porridge without salt. It says much for the men with him and the rest of the population, desperate and poor under the constant harassment of the British Army soldiers, that no one came forward to claim the reward that had been put on the Prince's head. This was 30,000 pounds, a truly incredible sum of money for most people and equivalent to many millions today. Yet no one would betray the Prince, even those who had not supported him overtly. Nor would any of the local population betray Pitsligo.

Living rough in the hills was hard on him. At one point he was forced to hide out under a bridge for several days, and on several occasions seeing patrols of dragoons, all he could do was lie down in the moss and heather, not having the strength to try and get away. One time he was sitting by the roadside not far from the Buchan coast when a patrol came by. He had by now not slept in a bed for months and was racked with coughing. He had long given up his fine clothes and was dressed in the simple hodden grey of the common folk of Scotland when one of the dragoons, passing him on the road and taking him for a beggar, threw him a handful of coins. This he gladly took and headed to a nearby inn for a warming meal. Contact with his wife and family was sporadic and he lived in great uncertainty from day to day. However he slowly got closer to his home and soon found himself among friends, for a while inhabiting a cave overlooking the Pentland Firth where at least he was fed regularly by a young lass from the neighbouring farm. Her father, although he hadn't come out in the rebellion himself, was a loyal tenant of Forbes. One day, Forbes took a risk and went down to the farm. He was sitting warming himself by the fire when there was the sound of horses outside. The woman of the house ran to the door just as it flew open. There stood an officer of dragoons,

'Right, woman, I know that damned rebel Pitsligo is hiding in a cave near here,' he said, 'if you know what's good for you, you will tell me right now where it is.'

The goodwife just looked at the soldier and said, 'Och all right,' and pointing to Pitsligo she went on, 'this poor old travelling mannie will show you where the cave is. It isn't far,'

And Pitsligo got up, coughed a couple of times, and shuffled slowly along the path on the cliff top, leading the soldiers to his hideout. Finding the cave empty, the officer told him to be gone and hid his men as best he could in the hope that his quarry would return. Forbes simply headed back to the farm, but, unsurprisingly, he didn't linger long,

Although the hunt for him was still on, the numbers of troops searching for him fell away as time passed. By late 1746 he was able to live in some comfort in the farms and houses of a range of local people, though visits to Pitsligo Castle itself were still very dangerous. This went on for years after most Jacobites had been given indemnity, for Pitsligo was, as a man who had rebelled twice, destined for one sentence if caught by government troops – execution.

It was nearly ten years later and the country was returning to something like normal, though there were still many small garrisons of troops stationed around Scotland, when he had his last and probably most dangerous run in with the troops. Forbes was staying with a loyal and close friend at his house, which if not quite a castle was a sizeable stone built residence and provided a welcome level of comfort. Another guest at the time was a widow, Mrs Donaldson, who was the sister of the lady of the house. One night, she kept waking up from the same dream. In the dream, the house was surrounded by soldiers. After this had happened several times, she got up from her bed and went downstairs. She peeked out through the closed curtains of a downstairs room and saw a group of soldiers in the nearby trees quietly approaching the house. Her first thought, things having quietened down, was that the soldiers were going to the hen-house to steal hens – the reputation of soldiers has never been good in such matters. But she couldn't be sure. So she went back to the window and, peeking through the curtains again, she could just make out an officer clearly directing his men towards the house, but motioning them to keep quiet. This could only mean one thing. They had somehow found out where Forbes was and were coming to search for him.

There was little time, but she knew what to do. At once, she went and woke Pitsligo and ushered him into a room where another visitor, Miss Gordon had been sleeping. She was still in her bed as Pitsligo was led into the room and hidden in a small recess behind the wall panelling. By now, the soldiers were going through the house and despite the best efforts of the occupants to hinder them, they were searching every room. Eventually they got to the room where Miss Gordon was. Now, she was a woman in her middle years and as she sat up in bed with the bedclothes held up to her chin, one of the soldiers came in and lifted her chin roughly, clearly checking to see if she was actually a woman. With a grunt, he let go and turned to leave the room. Just as he got to the door, Miss Gordon heard Forbes begin to cough. At once she started coughing herself. The soldier turned but as she carried on coughing to cover the increasing noise from behind the panelling, he turned away and left the room. Soon the soldiers had searched the entire house and Lord Pitsligo was led back to his warm bed. By now his coughing fit had subsided and he smiled as he looked at his hostess and said, 'Their prize would hardly be worth their effort – just a poor old dying man.' But then he added something that illustrates just who he was and why so many people were prepared to risk an imprisonment or death to help him. 'Ach, could you see that those poor lads get some break-fast and a mug of warm ale. It's a cold enough morning and I am pretty sure they bear me no real malice in their hearts.'

He continued to avoid capture until at last the warrant for his arrest was rescinded in the early 1760s and he could return to live openly at Pitsligo Castle, where he passed away at the age of eighty four.

Son of a Hero

AFTER THE SLAUGHTER at Culloden on the 16 April, the British Army spread out through the Highlands on the rampage. No one was safe and many people left their homes and hid out in the hills, often with little or no shelter. The red-coated troops tended to concentrate on the settlements in the glens, most of them ill-at-ease when in the rougher parts of the mountains. This meant many families managed to escape their ravages, though no one has any idea of how many died through exposure and starvation up in the hills in the bitter spring of 1746. One family who headed into the hills was that of Donald MacDonell of Tirnadris, the hero of High Bridge, the first Jacobite victory of the '45. His first wife had died after bearing him three daughters and one son, Ranald. He had re-married and had two further daughters. His second wife, Beathag, fled into the hills with the six young children. Ranald was about seven at the time with three elder sisters and two younger half-sisters. On hearing of the activities of the Redcoats, Beathag realised that their home would definitely be a target for reprisals. With the help of her children, she gathered together all their cattle and sheep and, loading their few horses with as much bedding, clothes provisions as they could manage, they left Tirnadris and headed into the hills of Glenfintaig to spend the night. The next day, they headed south-east through Glen Spean to the shores of Loch Treig, keeping out of sight as much as possible. As they went they could see plumes of smoke in many directions where houses had been burnt. They camped out in the woods on the shore of Loch Treig, unsure of what was to happen next. After about a week, a man came upon them in the woods. Beathag gathered the children round her as the man approached. He was wearing Highland dress and as he came close she recognised him as one of the men who had accompanied her husband when he had left their home.

'Good heavens, it is yourself Angus Roy,' she said, 'I had been told you had been killed up at the battle near Inverness.'

'Ach no, Beathag,' he replied with a concerned look around, 'I managed to get away and come back home, though there were many that didn't. How are you coping out here in the woods?'

'We are managing,' she replied simply.

'I saw your fire from my own home on the far side of the loch. Luckily we haven't been visited by these damned, red-coated swine yet. Now look, why don't you all come over to my place. You can't be comfortable out here in the woods.'

'Well we have the beasts with us and I think it better not to move them where they could be seen,' said Beathag in a worried tone of voice,

'Well then,' said Angus, well aware of the need to be careful, 'why don't you and young Ranald and the wee ones come over for the night. The other girls can tend to the beasts and they could come over for a bit of a rest in a day or two,'

Reluctant to leave any of her charges behind, Beathag saw the sense in this. If she went to Angus' house she could try and make it down to her sister Morag's house, a couple of miles further on down Loch Treig to see how she was. So she agreed and went with Angus, taking Ranald and the littlest of her daughters, who was only about four. After a good meal, she and Ranald went off to see her sister. They arrived at Morag's house, only to find that she had come down with smallpox. Fear of infection meant that they didn't stay long, just long enough to realise that though she was badly ill, Morag in fact was not as bad as she had been and would likely live.

On their way back to Angus's place, Ranald began to complain of a sore back. Within minutes he was having trouble walking and Beathag had to half-carry him back to Angus's. It was obvious that something was badly wrong with the lad, he was boiling hot and in considerable pain. They feared the worst. Soon it was clear that he had been infected by the smallpox, and within a couple of days spent in a fever he went blind. For more than a week he was tended by his step-mother in a wee barn nearby. No one else was allowed close in case they too became infected. On the far side of Loch Treig, his sisters were still camped out looking after the beasts, undisturbed by the marauding bands of Redcoats. After ten days however, Ranald's fever broke and he regained his eyesight. In later years, Ranald said that the usual Highland treatment for all ills, *uisge beatha*, the water of life, what we now call whisky, was in very short supply and none could be found to dose him. However, he said 'I just had to get on with things as best I could.'

By now the area was over-run with British soldiers and as soon as she thought the lad fit enough, Beathag decided that the best course of action was to head for Rannoch Moor. This is a wild and rugged place with no real paths, dotted with lochans and pools, and had long been used as a hideout by the wildest of the clan raiders. It was a place the Government troops were reluctant to go, as its wildness made it an easy place to set up ambushes and those who knew it could disappear like morning mist if chased.

By now there were considerable numbers of other people living rough having been forced from their homes by the soldiers and a handful of others from back near Tirnadris joined the camp. All agreed with Beathag that the best way of keeping what they had, their cattle, sheep and horses was to get away to Rannoch. There were many people who had nothing and were starving. So splitting into two groups, they headed to Rannoch following the old secret trails used by cattle-raiding clansmen, or caterans, since time immemorial. Beathag thought it better to send off Ranald and his eldest sister, Isabella, with a distant cousin of her own who had turned up, while she and the others herded the stock. She was sure that her husband's heroics at High Bridge would mean the government were seeking out his family and she worried what they might do to Ranald as Tirnadris's only son.

As Ranald afterwards told his friends in the Borders, often enough on their road east they were within earshot of roaming groups of British soldiers who were looting and pillaging wherever they went. Luckily, Beathag's cousin was well-versed in the tactics of the old raiding traditions, and they managed to avoid all contact with government troops, though there were several uncomfortable nights before they came to Rannoch. On the way, they met the son of MacDonald of Keppoch, and his family. The meeting was brief as the others were heading north to a place they thought safe. Although people would help each other when possible, everyone was in the same desperate situation and the only imperative was survival. When Ranald's party got to Rannoch, they met up with Beathag and the others and they hid out for a few days in an old bothy built of stone and turf. There was enough rough pasture for their cattle and sheep and horses, but they had to be kept under close watch for it was all too easy for them to wander off over the moor never to be found again. They had not been there for more than a few days when Angus Roy turned up with his brother Samuel.

His first words after saying hello to them all were, 'Things have quietened down a wee bit around Loch Treig, and you could come back to my place for a while.'

So the following morning the whole group set off back to the west, Ranald riding on the back of a wee Galloway pony. After his illness, the journey had worn him out and he was hardly capable of walking. In the woods that same evening, they saw some Highlanders at a distance driving a herd of cattle up into the hills and decided it was best to stop where they were. Angus and the other men built a couple of rough wooden shelters against the rain, and they settled down, all the time keeping their eyes open for any troops. For a couple of weeks they lived in the woods, before returning to the shores of Loch Treig.

One day Ranald, who still had not recovered all his strength, was driving some of the cattle onto an island in the fast-flowing river Spean, when he lost his footing and fell. He was carried away by the power of the cold water. Luckily Samuel, Angus Roy's brother, was nearby and managed to pull him from the water, but it had been a close thing.

There was, however, one strange thing that puzzled Ranald at this time. The regular soldiers of the British army might have left the immediate district but just up on the other side of the river there was an encampment of Government Militia, Highlanders like themselves, but in the pay of the Hanoverian Government. Even more startling was the fact that Angus Roy seemed to be supplying them with food. It was only in later years that he was to find out that under instructions of Campbell of Achallader, a lifelong friend of his father's, the family of Tirnadris were, in effect, being protected from other government troops by these men.

By now, word had come that their home at Tirnadris had been burnt to the ground, so there was little point in trying to head back towards Loch Lochy. Beathag was still very concerned that Ranald should not be found and one day he received incredible news. Two men, dressed expensively in the Lowland fashion, arrived at the encampment on Loch Treig and Beathag said to him, 'Well Ranald, it is best that you go away from here, at least for the present. Your sisters and I will do well enough here with Angus Roy nearby, but you are to go with these two gentlemen to friends of ours, in the south.' Just then his uncle Ranald Angus, Beathag's brother, and a young man who could speak English turned up. He was to go with them. Although still only a boy, Ranald had been brought up with ideas of kinship and honour that made him realise that as the surviving male he was in effect the head of his family. It was imperative that he survive, if his family was to ever regain the lands and status they had once held.

So after saying a sad goodbye to his sisters and stepmother and thanking Angus Roy for all he had done, the young son of Tirnadris left the Highlands and headed towards Edinburgh. Here he was kitted out in what he thought of as English clothes finding the tight shirt and trousers and leather shoes both unfamiliar and uncomfortable. His father's status and reputation made him a lad of some importance, and he was shown round quite a few houses in the capital where the flame of Jacobitism still blazed, even if it was behind closed doors. Much of this was confusing to the young lad for even with instruction from Ranald Angus and others, he still had little command of English, and was further confused by the Scots spoken by so many people in Edinburgh. He was taken briefly to Carlisle before ending up at Traquair in the Borders where he was sent to school and taught English. Being young and bright, and now in a more settled environment he soon began to master the new tongue. Tirnadris had left instructions with his wife that he wanted the young lad educated and hoped that he would choose the life of a soldier. He had known how slim Prince Charles's chances were and thought that if anything happened to him, Ranald could become a soldier and he would perhaps in time have the chance to fight for the cause himself in later years. This was not how it worked out.

Ranald had been at Innerleithen for more than a year and was proving himself a good student when a stranger turned up. Yet again, it seemed he was to move. His travel companion this time was a man who was passing himself off as a wandering fiddler, a good cover for keeping in touch with Jacobite sympathisers al over Lowland Scotland and northern England. The fiddler took him over the border to Warwick Hall near Carlisle. This was the home of Francis Warwick and his wife Jane, who, like Ranald and his family were Catholics. Any concern they might have felt about supporting the Jacobite cause disappeared after the trials at Carlisle where so many Catholic Highlanders were hung out of hand. They were happy to agree to carry on with the lad's education and ensure that he was brought up in the faith of his fathers.

Having no children of their own, they raised Ranald as if he was their own son, and spared no expense on his education. In his mid-teens, to finish off his education, they sent him to France to a college in Douai and it was here that Ranald at last made his decision as to a career. He did not want to be a soldier but he would make his own contribution to the ongoing struggle. What better way to do that than to enter the priesthood? Like many mothers, Beathag would have been proud of his decision even as she realised that the line of Tirnadris would die out. However, it was not long after this that Ranald was struck down with a fever, and already weakened by his earlier fight with small-pox, passed away before he could be ordained as a priest. The efforts of his family and their friends to ensure his safety, and carry on the Tirnadris line by taking him to England had worked, but only for a few years.

Some other books published by **LUATH** PRESS

Luath Storyteller: Tales of the Picts

Stuart McHardy

ISBN 978-1-84282-097-1 PBK £5.99

For many centuries the people of Scotland have told stories of their ancestors, a mysterious tribe called the Picts. This ancient Celtic-speaking people, who fought off the might of the Roman Empire, are perhaps best known for their Symbol Stones – images carved into standing stones left scattered across Scotland, many of which have their own stories. Here for the first time these tales are gathered together with folk memories of bloody battles, chronicles of warriors and priestesses, saints and supernatural beings. From Shetland to the Border with England, these ancient memories of Scotland's original inhabitants have flourished since the nation's earliest days and now are told afresh, shedding new light on our ancient past.

Luath Storyteller: Tales of Edinburgh Castle

Stuart McHardy

ISBN 978-1-905222-95-7 PBK £5.99

Who was the new-born baby found buried inside the castle walls?

Who sat down to the fateful Black Dinner?

Who was the last prisoner to be held in the dungeons, and what was his crime?

Towering above Edinburgh, on the core of an extinct volcano, sits a grand and forbidding fortress. Edinburgh Castle is one of Scotland's most awe-inspiring and iconic landmarks. A site of human habitation since the Bronze Age, the ever-evolving structure has a rich and varied history and has been of crucial significance, militarily and strategically, for many hundreds of years.

Tales of Edinburgh Castle is a salute to the ancient tradition of story-telling and paints a vivid picture of the castle in bygone times, the rich and varied characters to whom it owes its notoriety, and its central role in Scotland's history and identity.

Luath Storyteller: Tales of Loch Ness

Stuart McHardy

ISBN 978-1-906307-59-2 PBK £5.99

We all know the Loch Ness Monster. Not personally, but we've definitely heard of it. Stuart McHardy knows a lot more stories about Loch Ness monsters, fairies and heroes than most folk, and he has more than a nodding acquaintance with Nessie, too.

From the lassie whose forgetfulness created the loch to St Columba's encounter with a rather familiar sea-monster nearly 1,500 years ago, from saints to hags to the terrible *each-uisge*, the waterhorse that carries unwitting riders away to drown and be eaten beneath the waters of the loch, these tales are by turns funny, enchanting, gruesome and cautionary. Derived from both history and legends, passed by word of mouth for untold generations, they give a glimpse of the romance and glamour, the danger and the magic of Scotland's Great Glen.

Story provided the children of the ancient tribes with their education, their self-awareness and their under-standing of the world they inhabited.
STUART MCHARDY

Luath Storyteller: Tales of Whisky

Stuart McHardy

ISBN 978-1-906817-41-1 PBK £5.99

The truth is of course that whisky was invented for a single, practical reason – to offset Scotland's weather.

Raise your glasses and toast this collection of delightful tales, all inspired by Scotland's finest achievement: whisky. We see how the amber nectar can help get rid of a pesky giant, why should never build a house without offering the foundations a dram and how it can bring a man back from the brink of death.

Whisky has a long and colourful history in Scotland, causing riots and easing feuds, and McHardy has gathered together stories which have been passed down through many generations, often over a wee nip. *Tales of Whisky* is a tribute to the Scottish sense of humour and love of fine story-telling.

On the Trail of Scotland's Myths and Legends

Stuart McHardy

ISBN 978-1-84282-049-0 PBK £7.99

Mythical animals, supernatural beings, heroes, giants and goddesses come alive and walk Scotland's rich landscape as they did in the time of the Scots, Gaelic and Norse bards of the past.

Visiting over 170 sites across Scotland, Stuart McHardy traces the lore of our ancestors, connecting ancient beliefs with traditions still alive today. Presenting a new picture of who the Scots are and where they have come from, this book provides an insight into a unique tradition of myth, legend and folklore that has marked the language and landscape of Scotland.

Luath Storyteller: Highland Myths & Legends

George W Macpherson

ISBN 978-1-84282-064-3 PBK £5.99

The mythical, the legendary, the true – this is the stuff of stories and story-tellers, the preserve of Scotland's ancient oral tradition.

Celtic heroes, fairies, Druids, selkies, sea horses, magicians, giants and Viking invaders – these tales have been told round campfires for centuries and are now told here today. Some of George Macpherson's stories are over 2,500 years old. Strands of these timeless tales cross over and interweave to create a delicate tapestry of Highland Scotland as depicted by its myths and legends.

Out of Mouth of the Morning: Tales of the Celt

David Campbell

ISBN 978 1906307 93 6 PBK £8.99

How did the warlords of the Celtic Kingdoms combine ferocity with compassion?

How did the druids lose their sacred power?

What is the dark origin of the fairy folk?

The Celtic lands of Scotland and Ireland carry a rich heritage of legend and lore: myth comes to life in tales of feisty saints, elite warriors, powerful fairies and ordinary folk.

Distilled by a master storyteller, *Out of the Mouth of the Morning* eloquently unfolds these tales for our times. They are a reminder of our primal relationship with the land and the connections between all things. The author skilfully traces the carrying stream of Celtic consciousness from its origins in ancient landscapes and tongues, to the men, women and stories of today. Deftly weaving the ancient with the modern, he illustrates the essential nature of the folklore of the Celts in today's Scotland.

Out of the Mists

John Barrington

ISBN 978-1-905222-33-9 PBK £8.99

In the earliest hours of the morning shepherds gather, waiting for the mists that conceal the hillsides to clear. To pass the time they tell tales of roaming giants, marauding monks and weird witches. Enter this world of magic and wonder in *Out of the Mists*, a delightful collection of stories which will captivate and entertain you while answering your questions about Scottish history and folklore.

Why did St Andrew become the patron saint of Scotland?

How can you protect yourself from faerie magic?

What happened to Scotland's last dragon?

John Barrington uses wit and his encyclopaedic knowledge of Scottish folklore to create a compelling collection of stories that will capture the imaginations of readers of all ages.

This book is an invitation to savour the essence of ancient peoples linked into a communal spirit by legends, and to retell the tales of the Celt.

This Celtic collection is drawn from various age-old sources, lovingly and lyrically retold by a master storyteller.
SCOTLAND ON SUNDAY

Details of these and other books published by Luath Press can be found at:
www.luath.co.uk

Luath Press Limited
committed to publishing well written books worth reading

LUATH PRESS takes its name from Robert Burns, whose little collie Luath (*Gael.,* swift or nimble) tripped up Jean Armour at a wedding and gave him the chance to speak to the woman who was to be his wife and the abiding love of his life. Burns called one of 'The Twa Dogs' Luath after Cuchullin's hunting dog in Ossian's *Fingal.* Luath Press was established in 1981 in the heart of Burns country, and is now based a few steps up the road from Burns' first lodgings on Edinburgh's Royal Mile.

Luath offers you distinctive writing with a hint of unexpected pleasures.

Most bookshops in the UK, the US, Canada, Australia, New Zealand and parts of Europe either carry our books in stock or can order them for you. To order direct from us, please send a £sterling cheque, postal order, international money order or your credit card details (number, address of cardholder and expiry date) to us at the address below. Please add post and packing as follows: UK – £1.00 per delivery address; overseas surface mail – £2.50 per delivery address; overseas airmail – £3.50 for the first book to each delivery address, plus £1.00 for each additional book by airmail to the same address. If your order is a gift, we will happily enclose your card or message at no extra charge.

Luath Press Limited
543/2 Castlehill
The Royal Mile
Edinburgh EH1 2ND
Scotland
Telephone: 0131 225 4326 (24 hours)
Fax: 0131 225 4324
email: sales@luath.co.uk
Website: www.luath.co.uk